CliffsNotes™

Dante's
Divine Comedy: Inferno

By James Roberts and Nikki Moustaki

IN THIS BOOK

- Includes summaries and commentaries for all 34 cantos

- Provides insight into some of the mythological references throughout the poem

- Illuminates the meaning of numerology in the Inferno and how Dante used it

- Orients you geographically with the visual aid of a map—see the concentric circles of Hell!

- Study the political climate of Dante's thirteenth-century Italy and how it is expressed in the Inferno

- Reinforce what you learn with CliffsNotes Review

- Find additional information to further your study in CliffsNotes Resource Center and online at www.cliffsnotes.com

Hungry Minds™

Best-Selling Books • Digital Downloads • e-Books • Answer Networks • e-Newsletters • Branded Web Sites • e-Learning

New York, NY • Cleveland, OH • Indianapolis, IN

About the Author

James Roberts has been teaching literature for over 20 years. Nikki Moustaki is a freelance writer.

Publisher's Acknowledgments

Editorial

Project Editor: Sherri Fugit

Acquisitions Editor: Greg Tubach

Copy Editor: Billie Williams

Glossary Editors: The editors and staff at Wester's New World™ Dictionaries

Editorial Assistant: Jennifer Young

Production

Indexer: York Production Services, Inc.

Proofreader: York Production Services, Inc.

Hungry Minds Indianapolis Production Dept.

CliffsNotes™ Dante's *Divine Comedy: Inferno*

Published by:

Hungry Minds, Inc.

909 Third Avenue

New York, NY 10022

www.hungryminds.com

www.cliffsnotes.com

Library of Congress Control Number: 00-107685

ISBN: 0-7645-8654-8

Printed in the United States of America

10 9 8 7 6 5 4 3

1O/QR/QS/QS/IN

Distributed in the United States by Hungry Minds, Inc.

Distributed by CDG Books Canada Inc. for Canada; by Transworld Publishers Limited in the United Kingdom; by IDG Norge Books for Norway; by IDG Sweden Books for Sweden; by IDG Books Australia Publishing Corporation Pty. Ltd. for Australia and New Zealand; by TransQuest Publishers Pte Ltd. for Singapore, Malaysia, Thailand, Indonesia, and Hong Kong; by Gotop Information Inc. for Taiwan; by ICG Muse, Inc. for Japan; by Norma Comunicaciones S.A. for Columbia; by Intersoft for South Africa; by Eyrolles for France; by International Thomson Publishing for Germany, Austria and Switzerland; by Distribuidora Cuspide for Argentina; by LR International for Brazil; by Galileo Libros for Chile; by Ediciones ZETA S.C.R. Ltda. for Peru; by WS Computer Publishing Corporation, Inc., for the Philippines; by Contemporanea de Ediciones for Venezuela; by Express Computer Distributors for the Caribbean and West Indies; by Micronesia Media Distributor, Inc. for Micronesia; by Grupo Editorial Norma S.A. for Guatemala; by Chips Computadoras S.A. de C.V. for Mexico; by Editorial Norma de Panama S.A. for Panama; by American Bookshops for Finland. Authorized Sales Agent: Anthony Rudkin Associates for the Middle East and North Africa.

For general information on Hungry Minds' products and services please contact our Customer Care department; within the U.S. at 800-762-2974, outside the U.S. at 317-572-3993 or fax 317-572-4002.

For sales inquiries and resellers information, including discounts, premium and bulk quantity sales and foreign language translations please contact our Customer Care department at 800-434-3422, fax 317-572-4002 or write to Hungry Minds, Inc., Attn: Customer Care department, 10475 Crosspoint Boulevard, Indianapolis, IN 46256.

For information on licensing foreign or domestic rights, please contact our Sub-Rights Customer Care department at 650-653-7098.

For information on using Hungry Minds' products and services in the classroom or for ordering examination copies, please contact our Educational Sales department at 800-434-2086 or fax 317-572-4005.

Please contact our Public Relations department at 212-884-5163 for press review copies or 212-884-5000 for author interviews and other publicity information or fax 212-884-5400.

For authorization to photocopy items for corporate, personal, or educational use, please contact Copyright Clearance Center, 222 Rosewood Drive, Danvers, MA 01923, or fax 978-750-4470.

Hungry Minds™ is a trademark of Hungry Minds, Inc.

Table of Contents

How to Use This Book

CliffsNotes Dante's *Divine Comedy: Inferno* supplements the original work, giving you background information about the author, an introduction to the novel, a graphical character map, critical commentaries, expanded glossaries, and a comprehensive index. CliffsNotes Review tests your comprehension of the original text and reinforces learning with questions and answers, practice projects, and more. For further information on Dante and *Divine Comedy: Inferno*, check out the CliffsNotes Resource Center.

CliffsNotes provides the following icons to highlight essential elements of particular interest:

Reveals the underlying themes in the work.

Helps you to more easily relate to or discover the depth of a character.

Uncovers elements such as setting, atmosphere, mystery, passion, violence, irony, symbolism, tragedy, foreshadowing, and satire.

Enables you to appreciate the nuances of words and phrases.

Don't Miss Our Web Site

Discover classic literature as well as modern-day treasures by visiting the CliffsNotes Web site at www.cliffsnotes.com. You can obtain a quick download of a CliffsNotes title, purchase a title in print form, browse our catalog, or view online samples.

You'll also find interactive tools that are fun and informative, links to interesting Web sites, tips, articles, and additional resources to help you, not only for literature, but for test prep, finance, careers, computers, and Internet too. See you at www.cliffsnotes.com!

LIFE AND BACKGROUND OF THE POET

Life and Background of the Poet

Dante was born in Florence in May 1265. His family was of an old lineage, of noble birth but no longer wealthy. His education was undoubtedly typical of all the youth of that time and station in life.

When he was only 12 years old, his marriage to the daughter of the famous Donati family was arranged, along with the amount of her dowry. These betrothals and marriages were family affairs, and Dante dutifully married her, some years later, at the proper time and had two sons and one daughter.

Dante studied at the University of Bologna, one of the most famous universities in the medieval world. There, he came under the influence of one of the most famous scholars of the time, Ser Brunetto Latini, who never taught Dante but advised and encouraged him. Latini appears in Canto XV of the *Inferno*.

When Dante was still very young, 10 to 12 years old, he met a 9-year-old girl at a prominent function. She wore a bright crimson dress, and to Dante, she radiated the celestial beauty of an angel. The girl was Beatrice, and there is no doubt that she was the great love of Dante's life, and the greatest single influence on his work. Dante loved her at a distance, and she was, most probably, totally unaware of Dante's devotion to her. He recorded this devotion in an early work *Vita Nuova (A New Life)*. Her name appears only once in the *Inferno*, but she plays an important role in *Purgatorio* and *Paradiso*.

Dante's public life began when he fought bravely in a battle at Campaldino in 1289. By 1295, he was completely involved in political causes, and was elected to the City Council that year. Florence, at that time, had two political parties: the Guelphs, who supported the pope as the ruler of the Catholic Church but believed that he should not be involved in secular affairs (that is a belief in the American concept of the separation of church and state); and the Ghibellines, who believed the pope should rule both secular and religious factions. As a member of the Guelph political party, Dante was sent often on missions to arrange peace between the two warring parties. His opposition to the pope's interference to the unification of all the various city-states often brought him to be at odds with the reigning pope.

While on a mission to Rome to arrange a truce between the two parties, there trumped-up charges were made against Dante: He was charged with graft, intrigue against the peace of the city, and hostility against the pope. He was fined heavily and ordered to report to the Council to defend himself.

Rightly so, he was fearful for his life, and he did not appear to answer the charges. A heavier penalty was imposed. All of his property was confiscated, he was sentenced to be burned at the stake if caught, and his two sons were banished with him. In 1302, he was exiled from his native city, never to return.

At first he joined other political exiles, but he found them too stupid and selfish. It is not known where he spent many of his years in exile, but he was often well received. He began his great poem, the *Divine Comedy*, and it attracted a large and sympathetic audience. Commentaries flowed soon and, he became very well known. One of his hosts was the nephew to Francesca, who appears in Canto V of the *Inferno*.

He died in Ravenna on September 13, 1321, and he was buried with honors due him. Several times during the intervening years, the city of Florence has tried to get his remains returned to his native city, but not even the intercession of several popes could bring this about. His opinion of the citizens of his city was clearly stated in the full title of his greatest work, *The Comedy of Dante Alighieri, Florentine by Citizenship, Not by Morals*. Dante still lies in the monastery of the Franciscan friars in Ravenna.

Background of the Poem

Throughout the Middle Ages, politics was dominated by the struggle between the two greatest powers of that age: the papacy and the Holy Roman Empire (HRE). Each claimed to be of divine origin and to be indispensable to the welfare of mankind. The cause of this struggle was the papal claim that it also had authority over temporal matters, that is, the ruling of the government and other secular matters. In contrast, the HRE maintained that the papacy had claim only to religious matters, not to temporal matters.

In Dante's time, there were two major political factions, the Guelphs and the Ghibellines. Originally, the Ghibellines represented the medieval aristocracy, which wished to retain the power of the Holy Roman Emperor in Italy, as well as in other parts of Europe. The Ghibellines fought hard in this struggle for the nobility to retain its feudal powers over the land and the people.

In contrast, the Guelphs, of which Dante was a member, were mainly supported by the rising middle class, represented by rich merchants, bankers, and new landowners. They supported the cause of the papacy in opposition to the Holy Roman Emperor.

The rivalry between the two parties not only set one city against another, but also divided individual cities and families into factions. In time, the original alliances and allegiances became confused in strange ways. Dante, as a Guelph, was a supporter of the imperial authority because he passionately wanted Italy united into one central state. In his time, the fighting between the two groups became fierce. Farinata, the proud Ghibelline leader of Florence, was admired by Dante, the Guelph, but Dante placed him in the circle of Hell reserved for Heretics. Dante's philosophical view was also a political view. The enemy was politically, philosophically, and theologically wrong—and thus a Heretic.

Virgil was considered the most moral of all the poets of ancient Rome. Virgil's *Aeneid* was one of the models for Dante's *Inferno*. It is said that Dante had memorized the entire *Aeneid* and that he had long revered Virgil as the poet of the Roman Empire, especially since the *Aeneid* tells the story of the founding of the Roman Empire. Furthermore, in Virgil's Fourth Eclogue, he writes symbolically about the coming of a Wonder Child who will bring the Golden Age to the world, and in the Middle Ages, this was interpreted as being prophetic of the coming of Christ. Thus in the figure of Virgil, Dante found a symbol who represented the two key institutions: the papacy and the empire, destined by God to save mankind.

INTRODUCTION TO THE POEM

Introduction to the Poem

Reading Dante for the first time, the reader faces monumental problems: another society, another religion (medieval Catholicism is not the same as modern Catholicism), a different culture, and a different political system, where politics controlled the papacy, and the papacy was manipulating the politics of the times—and often the pope was a political appointment.

The Structure

The physical aspect of Hell is a gigantic funnel that leads to the very center of the Earth. (See the diagram later in this section.) According to the legend used by Dante, this huge, gigantic hole in the Earth was made when God threw Satan (Lucifer) and his band of rebels out of Heaven with such force that they created a giant hole in the Earth. Satan was cast all the way to the very center of the Earth, has remained there since, and will remain there through all of eternity.

The sinners who are the least repugnant, or those whose sins were the least offensive, are in the upper circles. In each circle, Dante chose a well-known figure of the time or from history or legend to illustrate the sin. As Dante descends from circle to circle, he encounters sinners whose sins become increasingly hateful, spiteful, offensive, murderous, and traitorous. He ends with Satan, eating the three greatest traitors in the world, each in one of his three mouths, at the center of the Earth.

The Punishments

Dante's scheme of punishment is one of the marvels of the imaginative mind; at times, however, it involves a rather complex and difficult idea for the modern reader.

Each sinner is subjected to a punishment that is synonymous with his or her sin—or else the antithesis of that sin. For example, the Misers and the Spendthrifts are in Circle IV. Their sins were that they worshipped money so much that they hoarded it, or the opposite, had so little regard for money that they spent it wildly. Nothing is so antagonistic to a miser as a spendthrift. Thus, their punishment is to bombard continually each other with huge stones expressing the antagonism between excessive hoarding and excessive squandering.

Another example is the Adulterous Lovers. In this world, they were buffeted about by their passions; in Hell, they are buffeted about by the winds of passion, as they eternally clasp each other. Those who deliberately committed adultery are in a much lower circle.

The punishment of the Thieves is simple in that their hands, which they used to steal, are cut off, and their bodies are entwined with snakes or serpents, as were encountered in Eden.

Allegory and Symbols

We follow the guide and Dante through adventures so amazing that only the wildest imagination can conceive of the predicament. Is this allegory or symbols? Most readers are anxious to have a one-to-one correlation between a thing and its symbolic equivalent: That is, a red rose equals love, and a white rose equals chastity. Thus, what do the beasts symbolize? There are so many different interpretations of their symbolic significance that each reader can assign a specific meaning, but basically suffice it to say that together they represent obstacles to Dante's discovering the true light on the mountain.

As an allegory, it is both simpler and more complicated than the symbolic meanings. This is a man's spirit on a journey through life and all of the lives that could prevent him from attaining ultimate salvation and a union with the Godhead, the source of all light. Those who failed during life are seen, in the *Inferno*, suffering from their sins in life, and Dante is thusly warned to avoid each and every sin to achieve salvation.

A Comedy?

Dante called his poem a *comedy*. In classic terminology, a comedy is a work that begins in misery or deep confusion and ends in elation or happiness. In Shakespearean comedy, the play often begins in confusion—couples breaking up or separating, but ends with everyone finding the right partner. In other words, a comedy is not something one would laugh about, but a movement from a low state of confusion to one where all people are combined for the greatest happiness.

The Structure of the Poem

Dante, like most people of his time, believed that some numbers had mystical meanings and associations. He designed the structure of his poem using a series of mystical numbers:

THREE: The number of the Holy Trinity: God the Father, the Son, and the Holy Ghost. The number of parts of the *Divine Comedy*: *Inferno*, *Purgatorio*, *Paradiso*. The number of lines in each verse of each canto. The number of divisions of Hell. The number of days required for Dante's journey through Hell.

NINE: A multiple of three; the number of circles in Hell.

TEN: The perfect number is the nine circles of Hell plus the vestibule.

THIRTY-THREE: A multiple of three; the number of cantos in each part.

NINETY-NINE: The total number of cantos plus Canto I, The Introduction.

ONE HUNDRED: A multiple of ten; considered by Dante to be the perfect number.

A Brief Synopsis

At the age of thirty-five, on the night of Good Friday in the year 1300, Dante finds himself lost in a dark wood and full of fear. He sees a sun-drenched mountain in the distance, and he tries to climb it, but three beasts, a leopard, a lion, and a she-wolf, stand in his way. Dante is forced to return to the forest where he meets the spirit of Virgil, who promises to lead him on a journey through Hell so that he may be able to enter Paradise. Dante agrees to the journey and follows Virgil though the gates of Hell.

The two poets enter the vestibule of Hell where the souls of the uncommitted are tormented by biting insects and damned to chase a blank banner around for eternity. The poets reach the banks of the river Acheron where souls await passage into Hell proper. The ferryman, Charon, reluctantly agrees to take the poets across the river to Limbo, the first circle of Hell, where Virgil permanently resides. In Limbo, the poets stop to speak with other great poets, Homer, Ovid, Horace, and Lucan, and then enter a great citadel where philosophers reside.

Dante and Virgil enter Hell proper, the second circle, where the sinners of Incontinence begin. Here, the monster, Minos, sits in judgment of all of the damned, and sends them to the proper circle according to their sin. Here, Dante meets Paolo and Francesca, the two unfaithful lovers buffeted about in a windy storm.

The poets move on to the third circle, the Gluttons, who are guarded by the monster Cerberus. These sinners spend eternity wallowing in mud and mire, and here Dante recognizes a Florentine, Ciacco, who gives Dante the first of many negative prophesies about him and Florence.

Upon entering the fourth circle, Dante and Virgil encounter the Hoarders and the Wasters, who spend eternity rolling giant boulders at one another.

They move to the fifth circle, the marsh comprising the river Styx, where Dante is accosted by a Florentine, Filippo Argenti, one amongst the Wrathful that fight and battle one another for eternity in the mire of the Styx. Dante wishes Argenti torn to bits and gets his wish.

The city of Dis begins Circle VI, the realm of the violent. The poets enter and find themselves in Circle VI, realm of the Heretics, who reside among the thousands in burning tombs. Dante stops to speak with two sinners, Farinata degli Uberti, Dante's Ghibelline enemy, and Cavalcante dei Cavalcanti, father of Dante's poet friend, Guido.

The poets then begin descending through a deep valley. Here, they meet the Minotaur and see a river of boiling blood, the Phlegethon, where those violent against their neighbors, tyrants, and war-makers reside, each in a depth according to their sin.

Virgil arranges for the Centaur, Nessus, to take them across the river into the second round of circle seven, the Suicides. Here Dante speaks with the soul of Pier delle Vigne and learns his sad tale.

In the third round of Circle VII, a desert wasteland awash in a rain of burning snowflakes, Dante recognizes and speaks with Capaneus, a famous blasphemer. He also speaks to his beloved advisor and scholar, Brunetto Latini. This is the round held for the Blasphemers, Sodomites, and the Usurers.

The poets then enter Circle VIII, which contains ten chasms, or ditches. The first chasm houses the Panderers and the Seducers who spend eternity lashed by whips. The second chasm houses the Flatterers, who reside in a channel of excrement. The third chasm houses the Simonists, who are plunged upside-down in baptismal fonts with the soles of their feet on fire. Dante speaks with Pope Nicholas, who mistakes him for Pope Boniface. In the fourth chasm, Dante sees the Fortune Tellers and Diviners, who spend eternity with their heads on backwards and their eyes clouded by tears.

At the fifth chasm, the poets see the sinners of Graft plunged deeply into a river of boiling pitch and slashed at by demons.

At the sixth chasm, the poets encounter the Hypocrites, mainly religious men damned to walk endlessly in a circle wearing glittering leaden robes. The chief sinner here, Caiaphas, is crucified on the ground, and all of the other sinners must step on him to pass.

Two Jovial friars tell the poets the way to the seventh chasm, where the Thieves have their hands cut off and spend eternity among vipers that transform them into serpents by biting them. They, in turn, must bite another sinner to take back a human form.

At the eighth chasm Dante sees many flames that conceal the souls of the Evil Counselors. Dante speaks to Ulysses, who gives him an account of his death.

At the ninth chasm, the poets see a mass of horribly mutilated bodies. They were the sowers of discord, such as Mahomet. They are walking in a circle. By the time they come around the circle, their wounds knit, only to be opened again and again. They arrive at the tenth chasm the Falsifiers. Here they see the sinners afflicted with terrible plagues, some unable to move, some picking scabs off of one another.

They arrive at the Circle IX. It is comprised of a giant frozen lake, Cocytus, in which the sinners are stuck. As they approach the well of circle nine, Dante believes that he sees towers in the distance, which turn out to be the Giants. One of the Giants, Antaeus, takes the poets on his palm and gently places them at the bottom of the well.

Circle IX is composed of four rounds, each housing sinners, according to the severity of their sin. In the first round, Caina, the sinners are frozen up to their necks in ice.

In the second round, Antenora, the sinners are frozen closer to their heads. Here, Dante accidentally kicks a traitor in the head, and when the traitor will not tell him his name, Dante treats him savagely. Dante hears the terrible story of Count Ugolino, who is gnawing the head and neck of Archbishop Ruggieri, due to Ruggieri's treacherous treatment of him in the upper world.

In the third round, Ptolomea, where the Traitors to Guests reside, Dante speaks with a soul who begs him to take the ice visors, formed from tears, out of his eyes. Dante promises to do so, but after hearing his story refuses.

The fourth round of Circle IX, and the very final pit of Hell, Judecca, houses the Traitors to Their Masters, who are completely covered and fixed in the ice, and Satan, who is fixed waist deep in the ice and has three heads, each of which is chewing a traitor: Judas, Brutus, and Cassius.

The poets climb Satan's side, passing the center of gravity, and find themselves at the edge of the river Lethe, ready to make the long journey to the upper world. They enter the upper world just before dawn on Easter Sunday, and they see the stars overhead.

List of Characters

Dante   A thirty-five-year-old man, spiritually lost and wandering away from the True Way—the path of righteousness and of God. Dante has become weak and is in need of spiritual guidance. Luckily, a guide is sent to him and he embarks on a spiritual journey to learn the true nature of sin.

Virgil   A "shade" residing in the Limbo section of Hell, also known as the first circle. Virgil is a poet of antiquity, much admired by Dante, and the perfect guide for Dante's journey. He is said to represent human reason and wisdom. Virgil is a strong and competent guide but needs Divine intervention from time to time to complete the journey safely.

The number following each name refers to the canto in which the character *first* appears.

Achilles (12)   One of the heroes of the Trojan War.

Antaeus (31)   Giant slain by Hercules.

Argenti (8)   Florentine, bitter enemy of Dante's.

Attila (12)   Chief of the Huns. Called "the Scourge of God."

Beatrice (2)   The inspiration for Dante's work. She entreats Virgil to save Dante.

Bocca (32)   Traitor of Florence. On one occasion he betrayed the Guelphs and caused their defeat.

Boniface VIII, Pope (27)   Dante's bitter enemy.

Brunetto Latini (15)   Distinguished scholar, beloved friend, and advisor to Dante.

Brutus (34)   One of the conspirators in the murder of Caesar.

Caiaphas (23)   The high priest who influenced the Hebrew Council to crucify Jesus.

Capaneus (14)   One of the seven against Thebes. Defied Zeus and was killed by him.

Cassius (34)   One of the conspirators who killed Julius Caesar.

Calvacanti, Cavalcante dei (10)   Father of the poet Guido who is Dante's friend.

Guido   His son. The father inquires about him in Hell.

Celestine V, Pope (3)   Resigned the papal throne, thus making way for Pope Boniface VIII.

Cerberus (6)   The three headed hound: guards one of the gates of Hell.

Charon (3)   The Ferryman of the river Acheron in Hell.

Ciacco (5)   A notorious glutton: his name means "the hog."

Cleopatra (5)   Queen of Egypt; mistress of Caesar and Mark Antony.

Dido (5)   Queen of Carthage. She was Aeneas' lover.

Diomede (26)   Companion of Ulysses in his last voyage.

Donati family (28)   A politically powerful family who caused the split in the political parties.

Erichtho (9)   Sorceress who conjured Virgil's spirit to help Dante.

Farinata (10)   A prominent leader of the Ghibelline party who defeated Dante's party.

Francesca da Rimini (5)   Lover of Paolo whose brother slew them in the act of adultery.

Frederick II, Emperor (10)   Attempted to unite Italy and Sicily.

Geri del Bello (29)   Cousin to Dante whose murder was not avenged.

Geryon (17)   A monster who represents fraud.

Gianni Schicchi (3)   Aided a member of the Donati family in falsifying a will.

Harpies (13)   In mythology, birds with the faces of women.

Jason (28)   Leader of the Argonauts in their quest for the Golden Fleece.

Judas Iscariot (34)   One of the twelve disciples. He betrayed Jesus.

Mahomet (28)   Founder of the Islamic religion.

Malabranche (21)   Demons who punish the barrators. The name means "evil-claws."

Malacoda (21)   One of the Malebranche. His name means "evil tail."

Medusa (9)   One of the Gorgons. The sight of her head filled with snakes turned men to stone.

Minotaur (12)   A monster with a bull's body and a man's head.

Nessus (12)   One of the Centaurs, killed by Hercules.

Nicholas, III, Pope (19)   Successor to Pope John XXI; accused of Simony.

Paolo da Rimini (5)   Committed adultery with Francesca, his brother's wife.

Phlegyas (8)   Ferryman of the river Styx in Hell.

Plutus (7)   God of riches.

Potiphar's Wife (30)   Falsely accused Joseph of trying to seduce her.

Ruggieri, Archbishop (10)   Traitor who starved Ugolino and his sons.

Satan (34)   Also called Lucifer, Dis, and Beelzebub, he is the "Emperor of Hell."

Scala, Can Grande ella (1)   Dante's friend and protector in exile.

Sinon the Greek (30)   Accused of treachery during Trojan War.

Thaïs (18)   A courtesan who flattered her lover excessively.

Ugolino, Count (33)   Imprisoned with his sons and starved to death.

Ulysses (26)   Legendary hero of Homer's *Odessey*.

Vanni Fucci (24)   A thief who shocks Dante with his obscenity.

Vigne, Pier delle (13)   He was unjustly imprisoned for graft and committed suicide.

Map of Hell

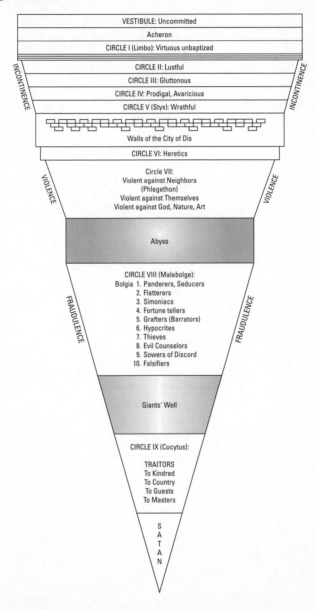

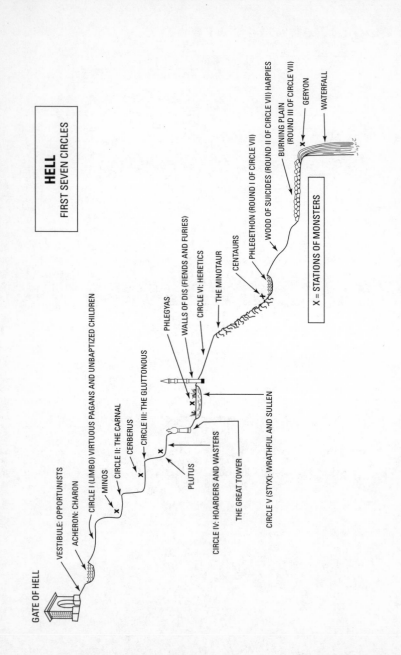

HELL
FIRST SEVEN CIRCLES

X = STATIONS OF MONSTERS

GATE OF HELL

VESTIBULE: OPPORTUNISTS

ACHERON: CHARON

CIRCLE I (LIMBO) VIRTUOUS PAGANS AND UNBAPTIZED CHILDREN

MINOS

CIRCLE II: THE CARNAL

CERBERUS

CIRCLE III: THE GLUTTONOUS

PLUTUS

CIRCLE IV: HOARDERS AND WASTERS

THE GREAT TOWER

CIRCLE V (STYX): WRATHFUL AND SULLEN

PHLEGYAS

WALLS OF DIS (FIENDS AND FURIES)

CIRCLE VI: HERETICS

THE MINOTAUR

CENTAURS

PHLEGETHON (ROUND I OF CIRCLE VII)

WOOD OF SUICIDES (ROUND II OF CIRCLE VII) HARPIES

BURNING PLAIN (ROUND III OF CIRCLE VII)

GERYON

WATERFALL

CRITICAL COMMENTARIES

Canto I

Summary

In the middle of the journey of his life, Dante finds himself lost in a dark wood, and he cannot find the straight path. He cannot remember how he wandered away from his true path that he should be following, but he is in a fearful place, impenetrable and wild.

He looks up from this dismal valley and sees the sun shining on the hilltop. After resting for a moment, he begins to climb the hill towards the light, but he is suddenly confronted by a leopard, which blocks his way and he turns to evade it. Then a hungry lion appears more fearful than the leopard, but a "she-wolf" comes forward and drives Dante back down into the darkness of the valley.

Just as Dante begins to feel hopeless in his plight, a figure approaches him. It has difficulty speaking, as though it had not spoken for a long time. At first Dante is afraid, but then implores it for help, whether it be man or spirit. It answered: "not a man now, but once I was." It is the shade of Virgil, who wrote the *Aeneid*, and lived in the times of the "lying and false gods."

Dante hails Virgil as his master and the inspiration for all poets. When Virgil hears how Dante was driven back by the "she-wolf," he tells Dante that he must go another way because the she-wolf snares and kills all things. However, Virgil prophesies that someday, a marvelous greyhound, whose food is wisdom, love, and courage, will come from the nation between "Feltro and Feltro," and save Italy, chasing the she-wolf back to Hell.

Virgil commands Dante to follow him and see the horrible sights of the damned in Hell, the hope of those doing penance in Purgatory, and, if he so desires, the realm of the blessed in Paradise. Another guide will take him to this last realm, which Dante cannot (or may not) enter. Dante readily agrees, and the two poets begin their long journey.

Commentary

This opening canto is an introduction to the entire *Divine Comedy*. This is made clear in the closing lines, when Virgil tells Dante that he can guide him only so far towards Paradise, and then another guide will have to take over because Virgil, being born before the birth of Jesus Christ, cannot ever be admitted to the "Blessed Realms."

The opening lines suggest first a realistic journey through a strange and eerie place, but after the first tercet (three lines), it is apparent that everything will be in terms of an allegory. It is a story of Dante's journey through life to salvation.

It begins when Dante is halfway through his life—35 years old, half of the biblical three score and ten—and he has lost his way. When Dante speaks of having strayed from the right path, the reader should not assume that Dante has committed any specific sin or crime. Throughout the poem, Dante is advocating a strict adherence to medieval Catholic theology: Man must *consciously* strive for righteousness and morality. In its simplest terms, Man can often become so involved with the day-to-day affairs of simply living that he will gradually relapse into a sort of lethargy in which he strays from the very strict paths of morality.

For Dante, Man must always be aware intellectually of his own need to perform the righteous act. Therefore, Sin is a perversion of the intellect. Thus, when Dante finds himself in a "dark wood," he is speaking allegorically for any man who is not constantly conscious of the "right path." If every waking moment is not consciously devoted to morality, Man can find himself in a dark wood.

Throughout the poem, the classical poet Virgil stands for human reason and human virtue, two admirable characteristics in themselves, but alone they are not enough to gain salvation. Through his poetry, his high ethics and morals, and the mere fact that he, in his *Aeneid*, had already made a journey through Hell in the person of Aeneas, Virgil is the perfect guide for Dante.

Furthermore, Virgil's hoarseness is Dante's subtle way of saying that the high morals and strict ethics of the poet have not been fully appreciated in Dante's time—that is, he is not read as frequently as he should be. Likewise, he has not spoken to a mortal since his death, and thus is unaccustomed to talking. And it is a common belief that a spirit cannot speak to a human until that human first speaks to the spirit—a custom used by Hamlet in approaching the ghost of his father.

The three beasts have been so variously identified and understood as representing so many qualities, it is sufficient, as noted in the introduction, to assume that they are three obstacles to Dante's returning to the "straight path."

This canto, which is the introduction to the entire *Comedy*, sets the scene for the long journey of which the *Inferno* is the first part.

Glossary

True Way   the way of God.

holy hour   dawn.

sweet season of commemoration   Easter.

shade   the word Dante uses for spirits in Hell.

Lombard   a native or inhabitant of Lombardy.

Mantuan   from Mantua.

sub Julio   during the reign of Julius Caesar.

Augustus (Gaius Julius Caesar Octavianus)   63 B.C.–14 A.D.; first Roman emperor (27 B.C.–14 A.D.); grandnephew of Julius Caesar.

Troy   ancient Phrygian city in Troas, NW Asia Minor; scene of the Trojan War.

the second death   a soul's damnation.

King of Time   Christ.

Peter's Gate   here, the gate to Purgatory.

CANTO II

Summary

It is now the evening of Good Friday, as the two poets approach the entrance to Hell. But Dante wonders if he is truly worthy to make the journey: He recalls that Aeneas, and also St. Paul, made the journey, and he feels unworthy to be included in this noble group: "I am not Aeneas, nor am I Paul," and Dante is apprehensive.

Virgil reproves Dante for being afraid and assures him that there is great concern for him among angelic spirits, mainly Beatrice, Dante's beloved, who is now in Heaven. Virgil relates how the Virgin Mary's messenger, St. Lucia, sent Beatrice to instruct Virgil to help Dante rediscover the "Right Path" from the Dark Woods. Virgil says that Beatrice wept as she pleaded, and Virgil eagerly obeyed her instructions and rescued Dante, so they are ready to begin their journey.

Virgil tells Dante to have courage always because the three ladies of Heaven—Virgin Mary, St. Lucia, and Beatrice—all care for him. Dante is reassured and tells Virgil to lead on and he will follow.

Commentary

As noted in the last commentary, this is the introduction to the *Inferno*. In later parts, the *Purgatorio* and the *Paradiso*, Dante will invoke Christian deities to help him, but here he does not invoke them concerning Hell. Instead, he turns to the classical Muses, to Genius, and to Memory.

In his short invocation, he mentions two others who have gone before him, Aeneas and St. Paul. They represent Dante's two great concerns: the papacy and the empire. The "Chosen Vessel" is St. Paul, and the reference is to his vision of Hell, as recorded in a widely circulated work of the Middle Ages (the fourth-century apocryphal book known as *The Apocalypse of Paul*, which Dante had evidently read), and the empire is represented by Aeneas who descended into Hell to consult his father Anchises to learn about the future greatness of the Roman people and the foundation of the Roman Empire. This preoccupation with the papacy and the empire will continue throughout the entire *Inferno*.

Note that the name of the Virgin Mary is by allusions—that is, her name is never mentioned directly. Neither will the name of Jesus ever be mentioned in this unholy place—only by allusion. And while Beatrice is mentioned in Line 103, she is never mentioned by name again.

Glossary

Muses   the nine goddesses who preside over literature and the arts and sciences.

father of Sylvius   Aeneas.

Apostolate   the office, duties, or peroid of activity of an apostle.

Aeneas   hero of the *Aeneid*, written by Virgil.

Paul   St. Paul; (original name *Saul*) died *c.* 67 A.D.; a Jew of Tarsus who became the Apostle of Christianity to the Gentiles; author of several letters in the New Testament.

Limbo   in some Christian theologies, the eternal abode or state, neither Heaven nor Hell, of the souls of infants or others dying in original sin but free of grievous personal sin; or, before the coming of Christ.

Seraphim   any of the highest order of angels, above the cherubim.

Lady in Heaven   Virgin Mary.

Lucia   St. Lucia, messenger of the Virgin Mary, patron saint of eyesight; here, represents Divine Light.

Rachel   an Old Testament figure; here, she is said to represent Contemplative Life.

Beatrice   Dante's childhood and lifelong love and future guide through Paradise.

Canto III

Summary

Canto III opens with the inscription on the gate of Hell. Dante does not fully understand the meaning of the inscription and asks Virgil to explain it to him. Virgil says that Dante must try to summon his courage and tells him that this is the place that Virgil told him previously to expect: the place for the fallen people, those who have lost the good of intellect.

The poets enter the gate and the initial sights and sounds of Hell at once assail Dante; he is moved deeply and horrified by the sight of spirits in deep pain. The unending cries make Dante ask where they come from, and Virgil replies that these are the souls of the uncommitted, who lived for themselves, and of the angels who were not rebellious against God nor faithful to Satan. Neither Heaven nor Hell would have them, and so they must remain here with the selfish, forever running behind a banner and eternally stung by hornets and wasps. Worms at their feet eat the blood and tears of these beings.

Dante wants to learn more about these souls, but Virgil moves him along to the beach of Acheron where the ferryman, Charon, tells Dante to leave because Dante is still living and does not belong there. Charon tells Dante to take a lighter craft from another shore. Virgil reprimands Charon, saying that it is willed, and what is willed must happen.

Charon speaks no more, but by signs, and pushing, he herds the other spirits into the boat. The boatman strikes with his oars any soul that hesitates. The boat crosses, but before it lands, the opposite shore is again crowded with condemned souls. Virgil also tells Dante to take comfort in Charon's first refusal to carry him on the boat, because only condemned spirits come this way.

As Virgil finishes his explanation, a sudden earthquake, accompanied by wind and flashing fire from the ground, terrifies Dante to such a degree that he faints.

Commentary

While the inscription is over the gates of Hell, they first enter the vestibule, that place reserved for those who did not use their intellect to choose God.

The inscription over the gate of Hell has a powerful impact: "Abandon every hope, all ye who enter here." Dante naturally thinks this applies also to him, and, in the first of many passages that cause Dante anguish, Virgil smiles and reassures him.

The inscription above the gates of Hell implies the horror of total despair. It suggests that anyone may enter into Hell at any time, and then all hope is lost. Dante cries out that this sentence is difficult for him to bear. However, this condemnation does not apply to Dante, because, allegorically, he can still achieve salvation, and realistically, he is not yet dead so it does not (necessarily) apply to him.

Dante, in this early canto, is moved to tears and terror at his first sight of Hell. He continues to be moved until he learns, later, to be unsympathetic towards sin in any form. This is part of his learning process and his character development throughout the poem. Dante learns that sin is not to be pitied; however, this lesson takes him many circles of Hell to learn.

In Canto III, Dante sets up the intellectual structure of Hell. Hell is the place for those who deliberately, intellectually, and consciously chose an evil way of life, whereas Paradise is a place of reward for those who consciously chose a righteous way of life. Therefore, if Hell is the place for people who made deliberate and intentional wrong choices, there must be a place for those people who refused to choose either evil or good. The entrance of Hell is the proper place for those people who refused to make a choice. People who reside in Hell's vestibule are the uncommitted of the world, and having been indecisive in life—that is, never making a choice for themselves—they are constantly stung into movement.

This explanation is the first example of the law of retribution, as applied by Dante, where the uncommitted race endlessly after a wavering (and blank) banner. Because they were unwilling to shed their blood for any worthy cause in life, their blood is shed unwillingly, falling to the ground as food for worms.

Among the sinners are the fallen angels who refused to commit themselves to either God or Lucifer and stayed neutral. However, a refusal to choose is a choice, an idea Dante uses that has since become central in existentialist philosophy.

Dante spies Pope Celestine V, who "made the great refusal" of giving up the chair of Peter after only five months, thereby clearing the way for Boniface VIII, to whom Dante was an implacable enemy. Celestine preferred to return to the obscurity of non-commitment, rather than face the problems of the papacy.

Theme

When Charon refuses to take Dante across the river, he does so because his job is to take only the dead who have no chance of salvation. Dante, however, is both a living man and one who still has the possibility of achieving salvation.

Virgil's incantation, "Thus it is willed there, where what is willed can be done," is a roundabout way to avoid the word "Heaven," which is repeated in Canto V. In later cantos, Dante uses other periphrases of various kinds.

The shore of the river Acheron that serves as the outer border of Hell is crowded with more souls than Dante believed possible. These souls are propelled not by the anger of Charon alone, but by the sharp prod of Divine Justice, until they desire to make the crossing. Choosing to cross the river is their final choice, just as their desire for sin on Earth was also their choice.

Glossary

Acheron   the River of Sorrow.

Charon   the boatman who ferries souls of the dead across the river Styx to Hades; in *Inferno*, he ferries on the Acheron.

spleen   malice; spite; bad temper.

Canto IV

Summary

Dante wakes to a clap of thunder. He has been in a deep sleep for some time, so his eyes are rested. He finds himself across the Acheron and on the brink of a deep abyss from which he hears the "thunder of Hell's eternal cry." Virgil asks Dante to follow him, but Dante is wary because Virgil is deathly pale. Virgil explains that his pallor is due to pity, not fear.

The poets enter the first circle of Hell—Limbo—the place where virtuous pagans reside. Virgil explains that these shades (souls) are only here because they were born without the benefit of Christianity, either due to being born before Christ, or because the soul was an unbaptized child. Dante asks if any soul was ever redeemed from Limbo, and Virgil tells him that the "Mighty One" came once and took a number of souls to Heaven.

The two poets have been walking during this conversation, and they pass by the wood of Limbo. Dante sees a fire ahead and realizes that figures of honor rest near it. He asks Virgil why these souls are honored by separation from the other spirits, and Virgil replies that their fame on Earth gained them this place.

A voice hails Virgil's return, and the shades of Homer, Horace, Ovid, and Lucan approach the two poets. Virgil tells Dante their names and then turns away to talk with them. After a time, the group salutes Dante, saying they regard him as one of their number. The entire group moves ahead, talking about subjects that Dante does not disclose, and they come to a castle with seven walls surrounded by a small stream.

Dante and Virgil then pass over the stream, go through the seven gates, and reach a green meadow. Dante recognizes the figures of authority dwelling there, and as the poets stand on a small hill, Dante gives the names of rulers, philosophers, and others who are there and regrets that he does not have time to name them all. Prominent among the philosophers are Socrates, Plato, Cicero, Seneca, and "the master of those who know" (Aristotle). Dante and Virgil leave this quiet place and come to one where there is no light.

Commentary

Between Hell proper, the place of punishment, and the vestibule, Dante places the circle of Limbo, devoted to those people who had no opportunity to choose either good or evil in terms of having faith in Christ. This circle is occupied by the virtuous pagans, those who lived before Christ was born, and by the unbaptized.

Many of the shades in Limbo are not really sinners, but people who were born before Christianity. These virtuous pagans live forever in a place of their creation. The shades that Dante singles out, such as Aristotle, Socrates, and Plato, lived by wisdom and thought, not religion, or at least not Dante's religion. Therefore, the Hell that they reside in allows them to reside in human wisdom, but without the light of God. Most of the first circle is in darkness, though Dante allows reason to create a small light of its own. Socrates, for example, wrote that he envisioned the afterlife as a place where one would have discussions with great people that came before or that lived in the present. Therefore, Socrates gained his ideal eternity.

Thus, Socrates is in Limbo, discussing philosophy and ethics with the other great souls that are there. In other words, Socrates attained the kind of afterlife that he, as a wise man, envisioned as the perfect one. His afterlife is not punishment; it is the failure of the imagination to envision the coming of Christ and faith in the coming of the Messiah. Moments after Virgil arrived in Limbo, he records that someone "in power crowned" appeared in Hell and took from there the shades of all the ancient patriarchs of the Old Testament, who had faith that the Messiah would some day come.

Allegorically, the fact that these pagans lived a highly virtuous, ethical, or moral life and are still in Limbo implies that no amount of humanistic endeavor and no amount of virtue, knowledge, ethics, or morality can save or redeem a person who hasn't had faith in Christ. Likewise, if an individual has faith in Christ, they must be openly baptized and in a state of grace to avoid Limbo. For Dante, good works, virtue, or morality count for nothing if a person hasn't acknowledged Christ as the redeemer.

The religious theme is particularly apparent in Dante's question that asked if anyone had ever been redeemed from Limbo. Virgil tells Dante that a "Mighty One" came when he was new to the circle and took some Old Testament figures: "our first parent" (Adam), Abel,

Noah, Moses, Abraham, David the King, Israel and his children, Rachael, and many more. Virgil again refers to the Harrowing of Hell, Christ's descent into Hell on the day of his death to rescue these figures. Aside from this one instance, there is no choice or escape from Limbo. Christ, according to Dante, is the only redeemer, and without him, these shades are in Limbo for eternity.

There are also moments of extreme self-awareness in *Inferno*, moments where Dante the Poet intrudes on his narrative. Dante feels exalted at meeting his forefathers in thought and poetry: Homer, Horace, Lucan, and Ovid. Clearly, Dante sees himself as one of them, and they invite him into their circle. This shows a great deal of self-consciousness on Dante's part; he places himself among the great classical poets, thus suggesting that he is one as well.

The language in this section is remarkable because Dante elevates these souls and seems to have the highest respect for them; words such as *honor*, *majestic*, *master*, and *luminous* don't occur regularly in the rest of the text of *Inferno*. Dante clearly believes that good works, morality, and virtue count for something, but not enough to allow a soul into Heaven.

Glossary

Mighty One   Christ.

our first parent   Adam.

Canto V

Summary

Dante and Virgil descend to the second circle, this one smaller than the first. This is the actual beginning of Hell where the sinners are punished for their sins. Dante witnesses Minos, a great beast, examining each soul as it stands for judgment.

Minos hears the souls confess their sins, and then wraps his tail around himself to determine the number of the circle where the sinner belongs. Minos tells Dante to beware of where he goes and to whom he turns. Minos cautions Dante against entering, but Virgil silences him, first by asking him why he too questions Dante (as Charon did), and then by telling him, in the same words he used to tell Charon, that it was willed, and what is willed must occur. (The word "Heaven" is not used, here or anywhere else in Hell.)

Dante beholds a place completely dark, in which there is noise worse than that of a storm at sea. Lamenting, moaning, and shrieking, the spirits are whirled and swept by an unceasing storm. Dante learns that these are the spirits doomed by carnal lust. He asks the names of some that are blown past, and Virgil answers with their names and some knowledge of their stories.

Dante then asks particularly to speak to two sinners who are together, and Virgil tells him to call them to him in the name of love. They come, and one thanks Dante for his pity and wishes him peace, and she then tells their story. She reveals first that a lower circle of Hell waits for the man who murdered them. With bowed head, Dante tells Virgil he is thinking of the "sweet thoughts and desires" that brought the lovers to this place. Calling Francesca by name, he asks her to explain how she and her lover were lured into sin.

Francesca replies that a book of the romance of Lancelot and Guinevere caused their downfall. They were alone, reading it aloud, and so many parts of the book seemed to tell of their own love. They kissed, and the book was forgotten. "We read no more that day."

During her story, the other spirit weeps bitterly, and Dante is so moved by pity that he also weeps—and faints.

Commentary

Literary Device

This second circle is the true beginning of Hell and is also where the true punishments of Hell begin, and Minos, the mythological king of Crete, sits in judgment of the damned souls.

Circle II is the circle of carnal lust. The sinners are tossed and whirled by the winds, as in life they felt themselves—helpless in the tempests of passion. This canto also begins descriptions of the circles devoted to the sins of incontinence: the sins of the appetite, the sins of self-indulgence, and the sins of passion.

Minos, like the other guardians of Hell, does not want to admit Dante, a living being still capable of redemption, but Virgil forces him to do so. Among those whom Dante sees in Circle II are people such as Cleopatra, Dido, and Helen. Some of these women, besides being adulteresses, have also committed suicide. Therefore, the question immediately arises as to why they are not deeper down in Hell in the circle reserved for suicides. Remember that in Dante's Hell, a person is judged by his own standards, that is, by the standards of the society in which he lived. For example, in classical times, suicide wasn't considered a sin, but adultery was. Therefore, the spirit is judged by the ethics by which he or she lived and is condemned for adultery, not suicide.

Dante sees Paolo and Francesca and calls them to him in the name of love—a mild conjuration at Virgil's insistence. Francesca tells their story; Paolo can only weep. Francesca da Rimini was the wife of Gianciotto, the deformed older brother of Paolo, who was a beautiful youth. Theirs was a marriage of alliance, and it continued for some ten years before Paolo and Francesca were caught in the compromising situation described in the poem. Gianciotto promptly murdered them both, for which he is confined in the lowest circle of Hell.

Theme

For modern readers, understanding why Dante considered adultery, or lustfulness, to be the least hateful of the sins of incontinence is sometimes difficult. As the intellectual basis of Hell, Dante thought of Hell as a place where the sinner deliberately chose his or her sin and failed to repent. This is particularly true of the lower circles, which include malice and fraud. In the example of Francesca and Paolo, however, Francesca did not *deliberately* choose adultery; hers was a gentle lapsing into love for Paolo, a matter of incontinence, and a weakness of will. Only the fact that her husband killed her in the moment of adultery allowed her no opportunity to repent, and for this reason, she is condemned to Hell.

She is passionate, certainly capable of sin, and certainly guilty of sin, but she represents the woman whose only concern is for the man she loves, not her immortal soul. She found her only happiness, and now her misery, in Paolo's love. Her love was her heaven; it is now her hell.

Theme

In Hell, sinners retain all those qualities for which they were damned, and they remain the same throughout eternity; that is, the soul is depicted in Hell with the exact characteristics that condemned it to Hell in the first place. Consequently, as Francesca loved Paolo in the human world, throughout eternity she will love him in Hell. But, the lovers are damned because they will not change, and because they will never cease to love, they can never be redeemed. Dante represents this fact metaphorically by placing Paolo close to Francesca and by having the two of them being buffeted about together through this circle of Hell for eternity.

By reading the story of Francesca, one can perhaps understand better the intellectual basis by which Dante depicts the other sins in Hell. He chooses a character that represents a sin; he then expresses poetically the person who committed the sin. Francesca is not perhaps truly representative of the sin of this circle, and "carnal lust" seems a harsh term for her feelings, but Dante chose her story to make his point: The sin in Circle II is a sin of incontinence, weakness of will, and falling from grace through inaction of conscience. Many times in Hell, Dante responds sympathetically or with pity to some of these lost souls.

This canto clearly illustrates the difference in the two personae: Dante the Pilgrim and Dante the Poet. Dante the Pilgrim weeps and suffers with those who are suffering their punishments. He reacts to Francesca's love for Paolo, her horrible betrayal, and her punishment so strongly that he faints. Yet it is Dante the Poet who put her in Hell.

Glossary

bestial   like a beast in qualities or behavior; brutish or savage; brutal, coarse, vile, and so on.

Minos   *Greek Mythology*. a king of Crete, son of Zeus by Europa; after he dies he becomes one of the three judges of the dead in the lower world. In mythology, Minos is a compassionate judge. He refused to judge his wife Paesaphe when she had an affair with a bull, producing the Minotaur, because he had never been exposed to such violent passions. Dante ignores this and makes Minos into a stern and horribly bestial judge.

wherries   in this canto, the term suggests fast movement.

Semiramis   *Babalonian Legend.* a queen of Assyria noted for her beauty, wisdom, and sexual exploits; reputed founder of Babylon; based on a historical queen of the ninth century B.C.

Ninus   husband of Semiramis.

Dido   *Roman Mythology.* founder and queen of Carthage: in *Aeneid* she falls in love with Aeneas and kills herself when he leaves her.

Sichaeus   husband of Dido.

Cleopatra   *c.* 69–30 B.C.; queen of Egypt (51–49; 48–30); mistress of Julius Caesar and Mark Antony.

Helen   *Greek Legend.* the beautiful wife of Menelaus, king of Sparta; the Trojan War is started because of her abduction by Paris to Troy.

Achilles   *Greek Mythology.* Greek warrior and leader in the Trojan War who kills Hector and is killed by Paris with an arrow that strikes his only vulnerable spot, his heel; he is the hero of Homer's *Iliad.*

Paris   *Greek Legend.* a son of Priam, king of Troy; his kidnapping of Helen, wife of Menelaus, causes the Trojan War.

Tristan   *Arthurian Legend.* a knight sent to Ireland by King Mark of Cornwall to bring back the princess Isolde to be the king's bride. Isolde and Tristan fall in love and tragically die together.

Po   river in northern Italy, flowing from the Cottian Alps east into the Adriatic.

Caina   the first ring of the last circle in Hell, according to Dante.

Lancelot   *Arthurian Legend.* the most celebrated of the Knights of the Round Table and the lover of Guinevere.

pander   a pimp.

Canto VI

Summary

Dante awakens in the third circle of Hell, the circle of the Gluttons. A stinking slush falls from the sky and collects on the ground where naked shades howl and roll in the mire.

Cerberus, the three-headed monster, stands over those sunk deep in the slush. He barks furiously and claws and bites all within reach. These spirits howl in the rain and attempt to evade the monster. Seeing the two travelers, Cerberus turns on them and is silenced only when Virgil throws handfuls of the reeking dirt and slime into his three mouths.

The poets make their way across the swamp, walking occasionally on the shades, which seem to have no corporeal bodies. One Glutton sits up from the mire and addresses Dante. The shade is Ciacco, the Hog, and claims to be from Florence and to know Dante. The two speak, and Dante feels sorry for Ciacco's fate.

Dante expresses his sympathy, and then asks Ciacco the fate of Florence and why it is so divided. Ciacco foretells a future war and the defeat and expulsion of one party. He concludes his prophecy, and Dante asks where he can find certain good citizens of Florence. Ciacco tells him that they are much further down in Hell because they committed crimes far worse than his, and that Dante will see them if he travels deeper into Hell. Ciacco then swoons and falls unconscious into the muck.

Virgil tells Dante that Ciacco will remain as he is (in the muck) until the Last Judgment, and the two poets talk of the future life. Dante questions Virgil concerning the Last Judgment, and Virgil answers that, although these souls will never reach perfection, they will be nearer to it after the Last Judgment than before, and, therefore, will feel more pain as well as more pleasure.

They continued their course along the way still talking and saying much more than Dante will relate and then they came to a place for descending: There they found Plutus.

Commentary

Literary Device

Cerberus guards Circle III, and as in mythology, he requires a concession for each of his three mouths (this time the foul mud of the circle suffices) before he permits passage. With his constant hunger, Cerberus is a fitting guardian for the circle of Gluttons, who transformed their lives into a continual feast and did nothing but eat and drink, for which they must now lie like pigs in the mire.

Cerberus should be familiar to the readers of Homer and Virgil. In those works Cerberus had to be placated with some delicacy in each of its mouths. In contrast, Virgil fills each mouth with some dirty slime which is more fitting for the guardian of the gluttons.

In the intellectual progression down through Hell, Dante moves the readers from the circle of lust, a type of sin that was mutual or shared, to the third circle, which includes sin performed in isolation. The glutton is a person with an uncontrolled appetite, who deliberately, in his or her own solitary way, converted natural foods into a sort of god, or at least an object of worship. Therefore, the glutton's punishment is a reversal, and instead of eating the fine delicate foods and wines of the world, he or she is forced to eat filth and mud. Instead of sitting in his or her comfortable house relishing all the sensual aspects of good food and good wine and good surroundings, he or she lies in the foul rain.

Aside from brief mention in earlier cantos, Canto VI includes Dante's first political allusion, which takes the form of an outburst from Ciacco. The voice is Ciacco's, but the words are Dante's. Ciacco's prophecies are the first of many political predictions that recur in the *Divine Comedy* and especially in *Inferno*. Because the imaginary journey takes place in 1300, Dante relates as prophecies, events that already occurred at the time he composed the poem.

Note that the souls in upper Hell want to be remembered on Earth, while the souls in lower Hell are reluctant to even give Dante their names.

Glossary

Cerberus *Greek and Roman Mythology.* the three-headed dog guarding the gate of Hades; in *Inferno*, Cerberus flays and tortures the Gluttons.

Plutus *Greek Mythology.* the blind god of wealth.

Canto VII

Summary

Dante and Virgil enter the fourth circle and are stopped by the raging Plutus, but Virgil then chastises Plutus as he has chastised the monsters in previous circles. Plutus collapses, falls to the ground, and the poets pass.

Dante gets his first glimpse of Circle IV, the circle for the Wasters and the Hoarders. Their punishment is that they are rolling enormous weights at one another, the Wasters shouting, "Why do you hoard?" and the Hoarders shouting, "Why do you waste?" After they clash, the souls hurry their weights back again, only to repeat the action, all the while screaming.

Virgil mentions Fortune in his discussion of the shades in the fourth circle, and Dante questions him further. Virgil tells Dante about Dame Fortune, who spins the wheel of fortune and casts her decisions onto mankind. Fortune (Luck) was ordained by Heaven as guardian or overseer of the wealth of the world. Some persons and nations have a greater share of this wealth, others a lesser one, but the balance changes constantly. Fortune is the maker of her own laws in her own realm, just as the other gods are in theirs; no one can understand her, and she does not hear those who curse her but instead goes her own way.

Virgil reminds Dante that time has passed quickly and that they must descend to another circle. They cross to the other bank and find a fountain of strange, dark water, which flows in a stream down through a crack in the rock. Following this stream to the foot of the rocks, they come to the marsh called Styx.

In Styx, Dante finds people immersed in mud, striking one another with hands, feet, and head, as well as biting one another. Virgil tells him that he is looking at souls destroyed by anger, and that more lie under the waters of Styx, making bubbles with each cry. Virgil repeats their words, which cannot be fully understood. The souls talk of the sullenness of their lives, when they should've been happy in the light of the sun, and that they now live sullen forever. The poets circle the filthy marsh and at last come to a high tower that has no name.

Commentary

Plutus, mythological god of wealth and riches, guards the Hoarders and Wasters, (misers and spendthrifts). Plutus' words are untranslatable, though some believe that they are a kind of incantation to Satan. Again and again the monsters of Hell challenge the poets, and yet Virgil again upholds the holy decree that allows Dante to continue his pilgrimage.

Theme

Keeping with Dante's theme, the sinners in this circle, like the sinners in other circles, live eternally in a punishment that fits their sin. The Hoarders and the Wasters are housed together, constantly fighting against their opposite, never to win, just as they couldn't win on Earth. Retribution also holds true for the Wrathful, who spend eternity suffering in their own and other's wrath, and the Sullen, who spend eternity alone and joyless, just as they did in life.

The question immediately arises as to why Dante places hoarders and spendthrifts in a circle lower than the Gluttons. That is, why is hoarding and spending more horrible than mere gluttony? The Gluttons misused the natural products of the world, which, for Dante, was not as bad as the misers and spendthrifts who hoarded and had no respect for the manmade objects (that is, money and property) of Earth. The distinction, however, is not vitally important. What is poetically significant, however, is that these two types of people were opposites in life, thus the punishment for them in Hell is mutual antagonism after death.

Virgil's discussion of Dame Fortune explains why these sinners are placed below the Gluttons. Dame Fortune is one of God's chosen ministers, who doles out luck and misfortune in a preordained manner. The Hoarders and Wasters, however, believed that they could outrun her; thus they believed that they could outrun God.

Literary Device

Dante again takes traditional mythological figures and distorts them. The Styx is called a marsh; in mythology it was a river (the river of Hate), one of the five rivers of Hades, and its boatman was Charon. Dante rather fully describes the source of the Styx.

The Styx serves a double purpose. It separates upper Hell from nether Hell, and it also functions as the circle for the Wrathful. Because the wrathful people were hateful during their lifetime, they now reside in a river of hate. These people are divided into three categories. There are three different kinds of wrath: the actively wrathful, the sullen (who kept wrath inside and are choking below the surface), and the vindictive.

First is open and violent hatred, and their punishment is that they strike out at each other in almost any fashion; the second type of hatred is the slow, sullen hatred. The punishment for this type is that they choke on their own rage, gurgling in the filth of Styx, unable to express themselves because they become choked on their own malevolent hatred. Finally, the vindictive strike out at others.

Character Insight

Dante's character begins to change in this circle. Here the poets come to the end of the first section of Hell, that of incontinence, and move to the second section, that of violence, which begins in the fifth circle. Dante is less fazed by what he sees in the fourth and fifth circle than he has previously been in earlier circles. Dante is becoming able to see sin as something terrible, and he is progressively less likely to feel sorry for the sinners, though he does feel sorry for sinners in a later canto. The sinners in the first section went from those less likely to hurt another human to those that probably did cause harm to others. Such is the structure of Dante's Hell.

Glossary

Michael   *Bible.* one of the archangels.

Charybdis   old name of a whirlpool off the Northeast coast of Sicily, in the Strait of Messina (now called *Galofalo*).

Permutations   any radical alteration; total transformation.

Styx   The River of Hate; in *Inferno*, a terrible marsh where the Wrathful and Sullen reside.

Canto VIII

Summary

The poets are approaching the great tower when two flames shoot from its top, and immediately, another flame replies from the other side of the marsh of Styx. Soon after the signal, a boatman, Phlegyas, arrives, eager to take more damned souls deeper into Hell. The sight of the poets angers Phlegyas, however, and he begins raging. Virgil chastises him, and the poets enter the boat.

As the boat makes its way to the other side of the swamp, a soul rises from the slime and accosts Dante. The soul is Dante's Florentine enemy, Filippo Argenti, one of the Wrathful in the marsh. Dante and Argenti exchange words, and Dante wishes that Argenti receive further punishment. Virgil praises Dante for his comment, and says that Dante will get his wish. Shortly, other shades descend upon Argenti and tear him to bits.

The boat approaches the shore, and Dante sees the City of Dis where the fires of Hell glow. Phlegyas lets the poets off the boat, and they are immediately accosted by a group of shades that question Dante's appearance in their realm. The shades refuse to let Dante pass, though they say that Virgil may enter but not return to his own circle. Dante is afraid that he will never be allowed to leave Hell, and he cries to Virgil to remedy the situation. Virgil goes alone to the gate of the City to see if he can open it. He returns unsuccessful in his task, but assures Dante that a Great One is on his way to open the gate.

Commentary

Style & Language

Canto VIII is weak in construction. Too much happens: A signal is given, a boat appears, Virgil has a short argument with the boatman, Dante has a fierce argument with Filippo Argenti, and so on. Why Argenti is singled out for mention remains an enigma, but apparently, he was a bitter enemy of Dante's and reveals himself as a man marked by all the passions, hatreds, and loves of his time. Prior to Canto VIII, there was one circle chiefly described per canto; from this point onward, however, circles overlap, and Dante the Poet devotes multiple cantos to single circles.

Theme

The theme of politics also shows up in Canto VIII. In fact, the most important action in this canto is the altercation between Dante and the shade of Filippo Argenti. Argenti was a bitter enemy to Dante, and his family opposed Dante's return to Florence.

Character Insight

Dante's character is indeed changing, as his reaction to Argenti (wishing him to suffer beyond what he already suffers among the throng of Wrathful) shows this change. By wishing Argenti more harm, Dante behaves wrathfully, just as the sinners in the marsh behave. Nevertheless, Virgil praises Dante highly for this behavior. Dante no longer feels pity for the sinners and is becoming aware of sin and developing a righteous hatred for it.

Dante and Virgil move on toward the City of Dis, the capital city of Hell, where the sins of violence and heresy are contained. The mythological king of the Underworld (Pluto) is sometimes called Dis, thus this city is named for him.

Literary Device

Once at the gate to Dis, the damned souls are angered at Dante's presence, and they refuse him entry, saying that Virgil can come in, but only to stay. In this encounter, Virgil is unable to convince the shades to let Dante through. Allegorically, this trouble shows that even human reason and wisdom cannot overcome every obstacle and that divine intervention is far more powerful than anything a human offers.

Glossary

Phlegyas mythological king of Boeotia; son of Mars; thrown into Hell for setting fire to Apollo's temple because Apollo seduced his daughter.

Canto IX

Summary

At the opening of Canto IX, Dante, waiting outside of the gate to the City of Dis, is afraid. The poets have a few minutes to talk, and Virgil tells Dante of the time when the sorceress Erichtho summoned out a spirit from the lowest circle of Hell. Virgil reassures Dante, again, that no one can stop their journey and asks him to remain where he is, because Virgil will not abandon him.

However, the conversation is short because the angels rush back and slam the gates shut. Virgil returns to Dante, sighing because the fallen angels bar the way. However, Virgil tells Dante that an angel from Heaven will descend to open the gates.

Virgil listens intently for the arrival of the angel because he can't see through the heavy mist. He regrets that he and Dante couldn't enter the gates by themselves, but they were promised help, though it seems long delayed. Dante is alarmed and asks his guide, in a roundabout way, if anyone from the upper circles has ever made this descent. Virgil answers that he was once sent to summon a shade from the circle of Judas, far below here, so he knows the way well.

Three Furies spring into view, saying that they should summon Medusa to turn Dante to stone. Virgil cautions Dante to hide his eyes against the beast, placing his own hands over Dante's eyes.

A noise like a hurricane causes the poets to look toward Styx, and they see a figure crossing without touching the marsh. Spirits rush away from him, and he moves his left hand before him to dispel the fog of the marsh.

Dante recognizes the heavenly messenger, and Virgil asks him to remain quiet and bow down. The angry messenger reaches the gate, which opens at the touch of his wand. He then reproves the insolent angels for trying to stop what is willed in Heaven and reminds them of the injuries suffered by Cerberus when he was dragged to the upper world.

The poets enter the gate into the sixth circle, and Dante is eager to learn about the inhabitants of the city. Dante sees a countryside of sorrow, a huge graveyard with uneven tombs covering the plain. The tombs are raised to a red heat by flames outside of every wall. Moaning and sounds of torment come from the open tombs. Dante asks Virgil what sinners reside in the tombs, and Virgil answers that they are the archheretics of all cults and their followers. The poets then turn right.

Commentary

In Canto IX, Dante returns to his customary style and grasp of his material. There is a short passage of dramatic impact: Virgil, the fearless guide, stands pale and helpless, speaking brokenly to himself. His incantations and reason are useless against those who willfully dared to oppose Jesus himself, and Virgil is forced to ask for the help that Heaven promised. Allegorically, this episode is another reminder that human reason can't achieve salvation without Divine aid. Virgil, as reason, can't understand sin committed in full knowledge and with deliberate will.

Dante is also afraid, but he is sensitive to Virgil's feelings, asking in a roundabout way if the poets will ever leave Hell. Virgil assures Dante that he returned from the darkest lair. Here, Dante tests Virgil's suitability as a guide, and Virgil soon proves himself.

Glossary

Erichtho   sorceress written about by Lucan.

Judaica   the final pit of Hell; also, Judecca.

Furies   *Greek and Roman Mythology.* the three terrible female spirits with snaky hair (Alecto, Tisiphone, and Megaera) who punish the doers of unavenged crimes.

hydras   water serpents.

Erinyes   Furies.

Hecate   *Greek Mythology.* a goddess of the moon, earth, and underground realm of the dead, later regarded as the goddess of sorcery and witchcraft.

Megaera   *Greek and Roman Mythology.* one of the three Furies.

Alecto   *Greek and Roman Mythology.* one of the three Furies.

Tisiphone *Greek and Roman Mythology.* one of the three Furies.

Medusa *Greek Mythology.* one of the three Gorgons, slain by Perseus, who turns mortal humans to stone if they look at her.

Theseus *Greek legend.* the principal hero of Attica, son of Aegeus, and king of Athens; famed especially for his killing of the Minotaur; tried to kidnap Hecate.

Gorgon *Greek Mythology.* any of three sisters with snakes for hair, so horrible that the beholder is turned to stone.

Stygian of or characteristic of the river Styyx and the infernal regions.

Arles city in southeastern France, on the Rhone; site of large, old cemeteries.

Rhône river flowing south from Southwest Switzerland through France into the Gulf of Lions.

Canto X

Summary

The poets begin their journey down a secret path in Circle VI, the circle containing the Heretics. Dante tells Virgil that he wants to speak with some of the shades in this circle, and Virgil answers that Dante's wish will soon be granted, as well as a wish Dante was hiding from Virgil. Dante replies that he had not been hiding any wish.

A shade rises from a tomb and recognizes Dante's Tuscan accent. Dante is at once surprised and afraid, but Virgil urges him to speak to the shade. Dante approaches the tomb and learns that the shade is Farinata, Dante's political enemy. Dante and Farinata exchange a dialogue that is simultaneously hostile and respectful. In the middle of their dialogue, another shade rises from the tomb that also recognizes Dante. This shade asks why his son is not with Dante, and Dante replies that it is because the shade's son held Dante's guide in scorn. Dante uses the past tense, "held," and the shade asks Dante if his son is dead. Dante hesitates, and the shade, believing that his son is dead, swoons back into the burning tomb.

Farinata, still standing in the tomb, continues his argument as if no interruption occurred. Farinata prophesizes that, "the face of her who reigns in Hell shall not/be fifty times rekindled in its course/before you learn what griefs attend that art." The two discuss the reasons for the split between the White and Black Guelph parties. Dante asks Farinata why shades can predict the future and Farinata answers that shades can know the past and see into the future, but have no awareness of what happens in the present. Farinata says that the ability to know the past and see the future is the light that the King of All (God) grants the shades.

Dante regrets that he didn't get to tell the other shade that his son is not dead, and asks Farinata to give word to him. Dante returns to Virgil looking downtrodden due to Farinata's prophesy, and Virgil tells him that the Sweet Lady (Beatrice) will make the situation clearer for Dante later. The poets bear left, passing deeper into the city with the flaming walls.

Commentary

The sixth circle contains the Heretics, those who believed that the body did not contain a soul. Many of these are Epicureans, followers of Epicurus, the Greek philosopher whose philosophy was the attainment of happiness, defined as the absence of pain.

Theme

Farinata, along with Cavalcante, is in the circle of the Heretics, partly because both he and Cavalcante were Epicureans. According to Dante's society, a heretic was a person who chose his or her own opinion rather than following the judgment of the papacy; Cavalcante and Farinata followed the Epicurean philosophy. The Epicureans believed that there is no soul, that everything dies with the body. They regarded the pleasures of life on Earth as the highest goal for man. Because Dante knew both Farinata and Cavalcante as Epicureans, he fully expected to meet them in this circle of Hell.

According to Dante's idea of retribution, the Heretics' punishment is to spend eternity in flaming tombs, until Judgment day, when the tombs will close and the souls inside will be sealed forever within their earthly bodies.

Literary Device

Dante consistently uses the act of prophesy as a literary device in *Inferno*. Farinata's prophesy for Dante, "the face of her who reigns in Hell shall not/be fifty times rekindled in its course/before you learn what griefs attend that art," means that Dante will also experience the grief of exile.

The other shade that interrupts Farinata is Cavalcante, another Epicurean, former citizen of Florence, and father of Guido, a contemporary poet and friend of Dante's. When Dante says: "Your Guido felt disdain," he could mean several things. He could mean that Guido, a modern poet, held Virgil and all classical poets in scorn and, apparently, held some of Virgil's virtues in scorn.

Note that Farinata and Cavalcante don't notice or recognize each other. Shades in Hell are not there for each other's companionship or compassion. They don't keep one another company, and they are more often together to provide more suffering for one another, as in the case of Ugolino and Ruggieri in Canto XXXIII, whose position next to each other for eternity causes pain rather than comfort.

Historically speaking, Farinata was a powerful personality of the preceding generation. He belonged to the opposing political party, the

Ghibellines, and the members of Dante's family were Guelphs. As Dante alludes to in this particular canto, Farinata twice led the Ghibellines against the Guelphs and twice defeated them. Thus, he and Dante should be bitter enemies. However, he is not someone whom Dante hates; instead, Farinata was a person that Dante admired tremendously. (A person can respect an enemy, even if they are opposed to him or her.)

Farinata's concerns are those of a warrior; any other sentiments are meaningless to him. He is a citizen, and he utters his request to Dante in the name of their homeland. Farinata is also a partisan: He first asks Dante about his ancestors. Likewise, he is an invincible warrior: He tells of scattering his opponents twice. Farinata's greatest glory was his love for Florence, a love that withstood every hatred and saved his beloved city. The theme of Cavalcante's paternal love, interwoven with Farinata's heroic love, is effective.

Dante created an image of Farinata as a very proud person, as well as an image of power, character, and strength. He describes Farinata as raising himself erect so that he could only be seen from the waist up, as though his upper body represents his total personality. This posture suggests that, spiritually, he towers above all of Hell and creates an image of infinite strength and grandeur.

Glossary

Jehosaphat   valley outside Jerusalem where it is believed that the Last Judgement will take place.

Epicurus   *Greek philosopher*. 341–270 B.C. founder of the Epicurean school, which held that the goal of man should be a life characterized by serenity of mind and the enjoyment of moderate pleasure.

Farinata   Farinata degli Uberti; famous leader of the Ghibelline party of Florence.

Guido   Guido Cavalanti, poet and friend of Dante; also Farinata's son-in-law.

The Second Frederick   The Emperor Frederick II.

Cardinal of the Ubaldini   a cardinal in Dante's time, said to be involved in money and politics.

Canto XI

Summary

The poets descend further and come to a group of broken boulders, behind which they rest a bit so that they can become accustomed to the foul stink that rises from the lower circles. Dante sees a headstone with an inscription, "I guard Anastasius, once Pope, he whom Photinus led from the straight road."

While resting for a moment, Virgil begins explaining the structure of Hell, especially that of lower Hell. Virgil explains that there are other, smaller circles, which comprise the last three circles beyond the wall that begins the sixth circle.

Circle VII, the next circle, is comprised of three smaller circles: one circle for Violence against Persons and their goods, another circle for Violence against Themselves (suicides), and the final circle for Violence against God, Art, and Nature. Virgil goes into detail about who resides in which circle and for what sins. Virgil says that God hates malice above all sins, and that is why Traitors are in the lowest circle.

It is growing late and they must leave for the descent into the next circle.

Commentary

Theme

Keeping to his religious theme, Dante again mentions the Harrowing of Hell. The rocks that the poets wait behind fell as a result of the earthquake on the day Christ died and came to Hell (the Harrowing) to retrieve a number of the virtuous pagans. Dante sees the headstone of Anastasius, the pope who gave communion to Photinus, and a deacon who was part of the Greek Church that denied Christ's divine paternity. Dante was probably confused on the history, however, because Emperor Anastasius was the person that convinced Photinus to accept the heresy.

**Literary
Device**

The geography of Hell is one of the most distinctive features of *Inferno*, and it is as meticulous as the structure of the poem. Virgil uses the waiting time, behind the boulders, to explain to Dante where the path they have been following will take them. This break in the action is a literary device that Dante uses to give a brief explanation of the structure of Hell.

The next circle, Circle VII, is divided into three smaller rounds that house sinners of violence, which are, symbolically, the sins of the lion.

The first smaller round features sinners against neighbors, murderers, and the makers of war. Dante makes no distinction here between the punishment of those who commit acts of violence against people and those that commit acts of violence against property. Hence, the first round also houses those guilty of arson, plunder, and extortion.

The second round of Circle VII houses those who sinned against themselves with suicide. The third and final round houses those who committed the sin of violence against God, Art, and Nature.

People in the third round are the blasphemers, sexual deviants, and the usurers (money lenders). Dante held usurers in great contempt, believing that charging any interest on a loan was a great sin. Art in this usage means industry, and Dante believed that industry should be the sole means of man's prosperity. To go against this plan was to go against God. Virgil says that Art is the Grandchild of God, meaning that Art is the child of Nature, and to act against Nature is a sin of violence against God.

Glossary

Anastasius   in *Inferno*, the leader (whether pope or emperor) who led Photinus to deny the divine paternity of Christ.

Photinus   deacon of Thessolonica who commited heresy by denying the divine paternity of Christ.

Sodom   *Bible.* a city destroyed by fire together with a neighboring city, Gomorrah, because of the sinfulness of the people: Genesis 18 and 19.

Cahors   a city in France known in the Middle Ages for its usurers.

sycophants   persons who seek favor by flattering people of wealth or influence.

Canto XII

Summary

The poets enter round one of Circle VII and must navigate a steep passage of broken rocks. They come upon the Minotaur, and Virgil taunts it into a fury, so that the two may pass unharmed.

Virgil tells Dante to turn his eyes to the valley where he will see souls boiling in blood. Dante sees a group of armed Centaurs galloping toward them. Virgil names them and tells a bit of their individual histories. One of the Centaurs, Chiron, moves his beard aside with an arrow and notes that Dante must be alive since he moves things that he touches, such as rocks when he walks. Virgil gives Chiron an explanation about their journey and asks that one of the Centaurs guide them to a shallow place in the river of blood where Dante can cross, riding on the Centaur's back. Chiron volunteers Nessus, another of the Centaurs. Nessus explains that the souls boiling in the river of blood were people that were kings of bloodshed and despoilment. Dante turns to Virgil for guidance, but Virgil says that he will let Nessus guide at this point. Nessus goes on to point out the names of some of the souls in the river. Nessus explains that the river grows deep again on the other side of the ford, and he names some of the other souls punished there. Nessus leaves the poets at the other side of the bank and goes back the way he came.

Commentary

Theme

In keeping with Dante's theme of justice, the sinners in round one of the seventh circle are the violent against others, and they spend eternity boiling in blood, just as they were steeped in blood in life. The river of blood is called Phlegethon and the souls in it are standing in a depth according to their sin—the worse the sin, the deeper they stand in the river. Should a soul try to leave the river, one of thousands of Centaurs will shoot it with an arrow but only so as to drive it back into the proper depth of the river.

The Minotaur is a perfect guardian for the sinners of the seventh circle because of his bestial and violent nature. Dante distorts neither the mythological Minotaur nor the Centaurs in *Inferno*; he found them appropriate as they were for this particular circle.

Style & Language

Unlike the other circles, Dante does not choose a soul to speak with or to make an illustration of; instead, he simply names some of the sinners in the round and moves on.

Theme

However, among the sinners are some of the most violent men in Dante's estimation, and two of them are of the Ghibelline party, the party in opposition to that of Dante's political party, the Guelphs. Dante again uses his divine narrative to make a political statement. In fact, rarely does a Ghibelline leader escape Dante's judgment.

Glossary

Slides of Mark near Trent   on the left bank of the river Adige about two miles from Roverto.

Infamy of Crete   the Minotaur.

Minotaur   *Greek Mythology*. a monster with the body of a man and the head of a bull (in some versions, with the body of a bull and the head of a man), confined by Minos in a labyrinth built by Daedalus, and annually fed seven youths and seven maidens from Athens, until killed by Theseus.

Centaurs   *Greek Mythology*. any of a race of monsters with a man's head, trunk, and arms, and a horse's body and legs.

Chiron   *Greek Mythology*. the wisest of all Centaurs, famous for his knowledge of medicine; he is the teacher of Asclepius, Achilles, and Hercules.

Nessus   Centaur who tried to abduct Hercules' wife and was killed for doing so.

Dejanira   Hercules wife.

Pholus   mentioned by a number of classical poets, but not much detail is known about him.

Alexander   Alexander the Great; 356–323 B.C.; king of Macedonia (336–323); military conqueror who helped spread Greek culture from Asia Minor and Egypt to India.

Dionysius   father and son, I and II, tyrants of Sicily.

Azzolinao   cruel Ghibelline tyrant.

Opizzo da Esti   cruel Ghibelline tyrant.

That one before God's Altar pierced a heart   Guy de Montfort, leader of a rebellion against Henry III.

Sextus   the younger son of Pompeii the Great.

Pyrrhus   either the son of Achilles or the king of Epirus; both were bloodthirsty warriors.

Attila   king of the Huns and called "Scourge of God" because of his cruelty.

Rinier da Corneto   bloodthirsty robber barron of the thirteenth century.

Rinier Pazzo   bloodthirsty robber barron of the thirteenth century.

Canto XIII

Summary

Virgil and Dante now enter into a pathless wood. This is a dismal wood of strange black leaves, misshapen branches, and poisonous branches barren of fruit. The Harpies nest here, feeding on the branches of the gnarled trees.

Virgil explains that this is the second round of the seventh circle, where Dante will see things that will cause him to doubt Virgil's words. Dante has already heard cries, but he cannot find where they come from and in confusion stops where he is. He believes that Virgil knows his thoughts: The spirits making such an outcry are hiding among the trees. Virgil tells him only to break off any branch, and he will see that he is mistaken in his thought.

Dante pulls a small branch off from a large thorn tree, and a voice asks Dante: "Why dost thou break and tear me?" Blood comes from the tree, and with it the voice, which asks if Dante has no pity. The voice continues, saying that all of these trees were once men and that Dante should have mercy upon them. Dante drops the branch, and Virgil tells the tree-spirit that if Dante had believed what Virgil had once written, this would not have happened. Since Dante could not believe, Virgil had asked him to pull off the branch, though it grieved Virgil to wound the spirit.

In compensation for this wound, Virgil asks the spirit to tell Dante his story so that he may repeat it when he returns to Earth. The spirit, moved by his words, tells his story.

He, as minister to Frederick II, was absolutely faithful and honest to him, but the envy of the court (they could not bribe him) turned Frederick against him. Because he could not bear to lose this trust, in sorrow he killed himself. He swears that he was faithful to the end and asks Dante to tell his true story when he returns to the upper world.

Virgil tells Dante to question the spirit if he wishes, but Dante is too sorrowful and asks Virgil to say the things Dante wishes to know. Virgil, therefore, asks how the souls are bound into these gnarled trees and if any ever regains freedom.

The imprisoned spirit replies that when the soul is torn from the body by suicide, it is sent by Minos to the seventh circle, where it falls to the ground, sprouts, and grows. The Harpies eat its leaves, giving it great pain. The spirits will all be called to the Last Judgment and will reclaim the mortal bodies forsaken by them. However, they will never regain their immortal souls that they took from themselves and will remain forever trapped in this strange wood.

The two poets now hear a noise like a hunt crashing through a forest, and two spirits appear. The second flings himself into a bush, but is quickly caught and torn apart by the pursuing hounds who carry him off.

Dante and Virgil approach the bush, which is complaining loudly that the fleeing spirit gained nothing by choosing it for a hiding place. Virgil asks this spirit who he was, but in answering, it first asks that they gather up all the leaves which have been torn off in the hunt and then says only that he was a citizen of Florence who hanged himself on his own door transom.

Commentary

The meaning of the punishment of the suicides is evident: In Hell, those who on Earth deprived themselves of their bodies are deprived of human form. At the Last Judgment the suicides will rise, like all the other souls, to claim their bodies, but they will never wear them. Their bodies will remain suspended on the trees which enclose the spirits of their owners.

One of the greatest changes brought on by the advent of Christianity is the change that took place in judging the suicide. In classical times, when a person could no longer live in freedom, or heroically, it was considered a stoic virtue to die by one's own hand. The last great act that a person could perform was to take his or her own life, which was the last free choice that person could make.

With the coming of Christianity, however, Jesus preached the concept that a man is free inwardly, and no amount of imprisonment or disgrace could destroy one's spiritual self. Thus, where the suicide was a virtue in the ancient days, for the Christian, it became one of the cardinal sins; murdering the body that God gave unto one.

Dante is naturally very confused when he arrives at the wood of suicides and hears human sounds but sees no human forms. Consequently, Virgil has to do something that seems extremely cruel. He has Dante pick off a branch from one of the trees, which causes the tree to bleed. Dante has previously shown that he is a person of infinite pity; therefore, the words of the tree evoke an unexpected response—surprise and sympathy.

The story of Pier delle Vigne is related so that Dante, on his return to Earth, can justify the man's loyalty—though not his suicide. The greatness of the episode comes when Pier delle Vigne says that to make himself a just individual, he has made himself forever unjust, by one stroke of the knife. Here is a gentleman, a man of honesty, elegance, and breeding; a cultured and intellectual man; and a poet, who has condemned himself forever to damnation and cut off all hope of repentance, by a single act.

This is one of the great poetic concepts in the *Inferno*. The spirit is not seen as a mean or evil or vicious man. Instead, he is a man who, in a moment of weakness, has taken his own life. Most of the other characters in Hell have something despicable about them, but Pier delle Vigne rouses a sense of sympathy. He is a man of obvious greatness that in a moment of weakness of will, took the irretrievable action, and after a life of noble service and devotions, he is condemned forever.

The naked men pursued and torn to pieces by hounds are Spendthrifts, reckless squanderers, who did not actually take their own lives, but destroyed themselves by destroying the means of life. The difference between these sinners and the Spendthrifts of the fourth circle is that the earlier cases arise from weakness, and the later cases from a deliberate act of the will.

The Harpies were winged creatures with the faces of women and were symbolic of the whirlwind or the violent storm. They stole anything; hence, in the woods, they symbolize the violence of the suicide and the stealing away of the soul.

Glossary

Strophades   the island where the Harpies live.

Frederick   1194–1250; emperor of the Holy Roman Empire (1215–50).

Toppo   a river near Arezzo in Italy.

Arno   river in Tuscany, central Italy, flowing west.

through Florence   into the Ligurian Sea.

Canto XIV

Summary

Dante gathers the leaves and returns them to the bush, and the poets pass to the other edge of the wood. Here is the beginning of a desolate plain, and Dante looks fearfully about him. Many souls are on this plain, some lying down, some crouching, and some wandering restlessly. Flakes of fire fall on this desert, making it burn and increasing the pain of these spirits who were being punished for their violence against God. They try to save themselves from this rain of fire by waving it away with their hands.

Dante notices one of the souls lying on the ground raging, and asks Virgil whom the soul is. Hearing the question, the soul replies that he is the same now as he was when he was alive—still unconquered and still blasphemous. And if Zeus had thunderbolts to hurl at him forever, he would never succeed in subduing this shade. This is Capaneus, killed by a thunderbolt thrown from the hand of the angry Zeus. Virgil chastises the soul violently, calling it by its name, Capaneus, and then tells Dante that the soul is one of the seven that laid siege to Thebes. Capaneus scorned God when living and scorns him still. For his defiance and heresy, he is confined here for eternity.

The poets walk in silence at the perimeter of the sand until they come to a small rill, a little brook of red water, reminding Dante of a stream in Florence that prostitutes use. Dante wants to know about the stream, and Virgil tells him that the stream begins in Crete with the tears of an ancient giant that flow down into the hollow of the mountain's pit where he lives. These tears form the source for the rivers in Hell: the Acheron, the Phlegethon, and the Styx. Dante is surprised to come to this stream, and Virgil explains that, because of their course, the poets have not made a full circle yet and new things that Dante sees should not surprise him.

Dante asks about Phlegethon and of Lethe, a river that Virgil forgot to mention. Virgil explains that they have already passed the Phlegethon (the river of boiling blood) and that they will see the Lethe in another circle. He explains that the Lethe is the river where remorseful spirits wash away their guilt, the River of Forgetfulness. Virgil tells Dante to follow him closely along the edge of the stream, so that they can safely cross the burning plain.

Walking between two rounds, they reach a small stream which is so red that it disgusts Dante. Virgil tells Dante this is the most remarkable thing they have yet seen, and Dante asks for an explanation. Virgil gives a long and complicated explanation about the formation of these rivers and how they flow through Hell.

The poets then leave the plains, and Dante is warned to follow the edge of the stream closely to avoid the fire of the burning desert.

Commentary

The intellectual concept of Capaneus in Canto XIV is one of the great characterizations in the *Inferno*. The character of Capaneus re-emphasizes one concept of Dante's Hell—the person retains those very qualities which sent him to Hell. In classical times, Capaneus was a figure who thought himself so strong that not even Jove (Zeus, or Jupiter) could destroy him, but he was destroyed by the thunderbolts of Jove. For his blasphemy on Earth, he is condemned to Hell, and his first words to Dante are "Such as I was alive; such am I also in death." This emphasizes that he has *not* changed.

Although Virgil does upbraid Capaneus for his pride, Dante seems to be drawn toward this powerful figure who dared to defy the gods. There is a certain power in Capaneus' defiance, and even in Hell, he remains as he was on Earth—and has the blind strength to say so. Being condemned to death because of his pride and his blasphemy, in Hell he remains filled with pride and continues to blaspheme against his god. Capaneus is ultimately insulting and defiant by saying that Jove himself will grow weary of trying to punish him before he, Capaneus, will give in to Jove's punishment. This is the ultimate defiance.

Here the idea expressed is important throughout Hell: In any particular circle, the *degree* of punishment is not always the same. Capaneus is being punished more than anyone else in this circle, and according to Virgil, as Capaneus keeps blaspheming against God, his punishment will increase throughout eternity.

Glossary

Cato   Cato of Utica; also a friend of Cicero.

Alexander   356–323 B.C.; king of Macedonia (336–323); military conqueror who helped spread Greek culture from Asia Minor and Egypt to India.

Mongibello   Mount Edna, where Vulcan had his forge.

Vulcan   *Roman Mythology*. the god of fire and of metalworking; later identified with the Greek Hephaestus.

Phlegra   the battle at Phlegra for which Vulcan was the forge.

Bulicame   a red-tinted stream in Viterbo where the prostitutes bathed.

Crete   Greek island in the Mediterranean.

Rhea   *Greek Mythology*. daughter of Uranus and Gaea, wife of Cronus, and mother of Zeus, Poseidon, Hades, Demeter, Hera, and Hestia; identified with the Roman Ops and the Phrygian Cybele.

Corybantes   any of the attendants who follow the Phrygian goddess Cybele with dancing and frenzied orgies.

Daimetta   Egypt.

Cocytus   the final circle of Hell.

Canto XV

Summary

The poets begin walking along the high banks of the stream, protected from the snow-like flames by the steam that the boiling brook emits. A company of wandering shades comes into sight and they stare closely at the poets. One of the shades recognizes Dante and is overjoyed to see him. The shade is Ser Brunetto Latini, and once identified, he asks to walk with Dante for a bit because if he stops for even a moment, he will have to lay still under the flames for 100 years and not be allowed to fan them off.

Dante and Brunetto begin walking, with Dante up on the high bank and Brunetto at his hem. Dante explains how his journey though Hell came to be, and Brunetto praises Dante's work with the highest of words and gives him some advice, as well as a prophesy about his coming exile. Dante tells Brunetto that he wishes him alive again, that he sees him as a paternal figure, and that he feels deep gratitude for his teachings.

Dante speaks with great kindness and gratitude for Brunetto's past help and teaching, and tells him that he thinks of him often. Dante also says he will ask a certain lady about the prophecies and is prepared to accept what Fortune wills for him.

Dante asks Brunetto what other souls reside with him in this burning plain and is told that only a few can be mentioned. All of the spirits with him were scholars of renown, and all of them are guilty of the same crime—sodomy (even though Brunetto does not name it). Suddenly, Brunetto feels a calling and must return to his band. Before he goes, he tells Dante to remember his great book, the *Treasure*.

Commentary

The most significant moment in Canto XV is the meeting between Dante and Ser Brunetto, Dante's mentor and a source of encouragement. Dante was influenced by Ser Brunetto's works, one of which he mentions—the *Treasure*.

Character Insight

This is one of the high points in the *Inferno*. Clearly, Dante felt that Ser Brunetto was an important man and cared for him deeply. When he addresses him (in the original Italian), for example, Dante uses the respectful form of "you," something he does not do with the other shades. Brunetto Latini was one who understood Dante's genius when others failed to do so. Now the poet still finds in his master the support and the encouragement that he needs to withstand the attacks that his fellow citizens are going to direct at him. In Brunetto Latini, Dante finds a sympathetic fellow artist, especially since he encourages Dante to follow his (Dante's own) star to achieve the glorious fortune for which he is destined.

Dante consistently places men he respects in Hell, and he gives them the respect they are due in his meetings with them. However, respect and good deeds on Earth are not enough to survive damnation in Dante's ideology.

Literary Device

At this point in his journey, Dante hears the third of three prophecies concerning his exile from Ser Brunetto. Brunetto prophesizes that Dante shall be hungered for on both sides, meaning that both political parties (the Guelphs and the Ghibellines) will hunger to destroy him. This is hardly a real prophecy, considering that the events Brunetto warns Dante about already came to pass well before Dante wrote *Inferno*.

Theme

The symbolism of the rain of fire and the scorching sand is that of sterility and unproductiveness: The rain should be life giving, the soil fertile. Instead, symbolically, the sex practices of the sodomite are not life giving.

Glossary

Francesco d'Accorso   Florentine scholar.

Servent of Servents   Boniface VII, Dante's enemy.

Arno   river in Tuscany, central Italy, flowing west through Florence and into the Ligurian Sea.

Bacchiglione   river in Italy.

Canto XVI

Summary

The poets near a waterfall at the edge of the third round of Circle VII, and they can hear the rumbling of its water falling into the next circle. Three shades run to Dante, recognizing his Florentine dress. Virgil has a great deal of respect for these shades and tells Dante to speak with them. Because they are in the realm of the Sodomites and cannot stop walking, they form a circle and continue walking to speak to Dante.

One shade tells Dante who they are, and tells him that they should not be looked upon with contempt because of their present condition, for in life they were famous. Dante recognizes them and tells them that he has always had affection for them. Dante tells them of his journey. They wish him luck, and entreat him to speak of them in the upper world.

The poets continue toward the waterfall and Virgil asks Dante for his cord, which Dante wears around his body. Virgil tosses the cord into the pit. Dante expects a strange event, and Virgil reads his mind, telling him that an unusual event will indeed occur. Dante is astonished—surprised enough to swear on his whole poem—when he sees a strange shape fill the air.

Commentary

Canto XVI holds less interest, in comparison to the sincerity and sorrow of the preceding canto. Whereas the preceding canto was very lyrical and poetic, the allusions in Canto XVI are almost all politically motivated.

Theme

The three souls that Dante meets in this circle are all famous Guelph nobles and party leaders from just before Dante's time. During his life, Dante would have heard great stories about these people, and clearly their power and nobility follow them to Hell, or at least they continue their greatness in Dante's mind. No matter how powerful or worthy on Earth, even if a soul was on the same side as Dante politically, he could not avoid the fires of Hell. Dante felt that sin was despicable, so much so that even his friends do not escape.

Dante informs them of what is happening in Florence. As Dante draws closer to the end of Hell, he becomes numb to sin and sinners; he is willing to accept their fate.

The main dramatic action in Canto XVI is the tossing of Dante's cord into the pit. This cord seems to come from nowhere; it is not mentioned previously and there is no reason why Dante should be wearing a cord. Dante needed a dramatic device at this moment of the poem to aid in the calling of Geryon, who will deliver the poets to the eighth circle. He mentions that he hoped to use the cord at one time to snare the leopard with the gaudy pelt, one of the beasts from the beginning of the journey, which is the symbol of the Fraudulent and the Malicious (the residents of the Circle VIII, which the poets are about to enter). There is no definitive reading of the tossing of the cord. Certainly, the action functions to call the monster, which propels the narrative forward. Dante said that the reading of the *Comedy* should first and foremost be literal, which is a good enough reason at this point in the poem to say simply that the cord is a device.

Glossary

Guido Guerra a leader of the Guelphs; the last name means "war."

Gualdrada legendary modest woman, used as a model of womanhood.

Tegghiaio Aldobrandi a knight and a Guelph noble.

Jacopo Rusticucci respected Florentine knight.

Borsiere courtier arranger of marriages and a peacemaker.

San Benedetto dell'Alpe a monastery close to Florence.

Canto XVII

Summary

Geryon, the monster, lands on the brink of the abyss, his tail hanging over the side. Geryon's face is that of an innocent man, but his body is half-reptile, half-hairy beast, with a scorpion's stinger at the end of his tail. The poets approach him, and Virgil tells Dante to go and see the sinners in the final round of Circle VII, warning him to make his talk brief.

Dante moves around the circle alone and approaches a group of sinners whose eyes are full of tears and set on enormous purses hanging around their necks. Dante sees no one that he knows among the group, though he seems to recognize the coat-of-arm symbols emblazoned on the purses. This group, the Usurers, tells Dante to go away and leave them alone. Fearing that he has stayed too long, Dante goes back to Virgil, who is already mounted on the rump of Geryon. Dante is terribly afraid but mounts Geryon anyway, and before he can ask for assistance, Virgil embraces him and helps him hold on. Virgil tells Geryon to fly smoothly, which he does, and he lets the poets off at the bottom of the pit near the eighth circle. Geryon takes off like a shot, relieved of Dante's living weight.

Commentary

Like the beginning of the other two main sections of Hell, a familiar mythological monster rules the entrance of the particular souls in this sphere. In Canto XVII, the monster Geryon symbolizes Fraud, the sin of the souls in Circle VIII. Furthermore, like Fraud, his innocent face fools the onlooker long enough to be stung by his scorpion-like tail.

Literary
Device

Again, Dante alters the figure of a mythological creature from its traditional form (one of the poet's favorite literary devices), functioning to make Hell a place where traditional expectations may not exist. Geryon is the mythological king of Spain who was killed by Hercules, and he was traditionally represented as having three heads and three bodies. The figure of Geryon that Dante creates in *Inferno* is a consolidation of the Lion (violence) and the Leopard (malice), with its gaudy coat, recalling two of the three beasts that Dante initially confronted in the beginning of *Inferno*.

Character Insight

Dante the Pilgrim is indeed beginning to understand the true nature of sin as he confronts the Usurers, the sinners in the final round of Circle VII. He does not linger among them, insisting on their names, but coolly observes them and moves on.

Dante the Poet places these sinners in dire circumstances, and tells none of their names, hiding them from Earth, making sure that none were remembered. The faces of the Usurers lack individuality because their concern with money made them lose their individuality. However, the signs and symbols on the sinner's purses indicate their families. Dante hated usury, the lending of money, with or without interest, which is why these sinners find themselves in a deep circle under a powerful punishment.

Style & Language

As the sinners' sins become more vulgar and base, the language in the poem becomes more graphic, so as to illustrate the misery of the usurers. In this canto, the Usurers are described as dogs in summer, and their very nature and description is disgusting. The power of the language increases as the poem goes on, which Dante illustrates in later cantos.

Glossary

Tartar or Turk   Tartars and Turks were the great weavers of Dante's time.

Arachne   famous spinner who challenged Minerva to a spinning contest; Minerva became enraged at the result of the contest and turned Arachne into a spider.

Vitaliano   another Paduan.

quartanary chill   a four-day illness that includes chill.

Phaeton   Son of Apollo who drove the chariot of the sun and lost control of the horses, so Zeus struck him down so that the world would not catch fire; the track of the horses is the Milky Way.

Icarus   *Greek Mythology.* the son of Daedalus; escaping from Crete by flying with wings made by Daedalus, Icarus flies so high that the sun's heat melts the wax by which his wings are fastened, and he falls to his death in the Aegean sea.

Canto XVIII

Summary

The poets find themselves at the brink of Circle VIII with its ten "Malebolges" (meaning evil ditches or pockets or chasms), a cavern of stone with ten concentric Bowges (chasms or moats or trenches) dug into the rock in which the sinners of different natures reside.

In the first chasm (or valley), the poets approach the first of what can also be thought of as chasms or valleys, filled with tormented sinners walking in both directions. Demons with horns flog them continuously to keep them moving.

Dante notices a sinner on the side on which he is standing and calls to him. The sinner tries to hide his face, but is compelled to speak. He is Venedico Caccianemico of Bologna, who admits that he brought his own sister "the fair Ghisolabella 'round to serve the will and lust of the Marquis." He says that there are more souls from Bologna in the ditch with him than there are living in Bologna at present. A demon strikes him with a whip and orders him off.

The poets approach a narrow bridge spanning the pit, and Virgil tells Dante to observe the sinners walking around the other way. There Dante sees the proud Jason, seeming strong in spite of the pain he receives in the pit. Other seducers are with him.

Moving to the second chasm or moat, Dante observes groups of sinners writhing in sewage and excrement, and he again recognizes a sinner, Alessio Interminelli da Lucca, who suffers in this pit because of false flattery. Virgil points out a woman in the chasm, Thaïs the whore, who also resides in the chasm because of false flattery. The poets turn away from these sinners. They have seen enough.

Commentary

The poets have entered the circle of "Malebolge." As noted in the summary above, there is a certain amount of confusion over the terminology, which can lead to a confusion of images. The word "Bolgia" in Italian means both "pit" and "pouch," but neither term seems to be the best translation for the idea Dante wanted to convey. The words "chasm" or "ravine" seem to carry the connotation of depth and ruggedness that Dante would wish, but "moat" would probably be equally acceptable, as Dante implies in an early stanza. The word "well" might be replaced with "crater" or "abyss" in matters of clarity. And, the prefix of "Male" means variously "sickness" or "evil."

Malebolge is a terrible place, in the true meaning of the word. Dante has devoted thirteen cantos to this one circle of Hell. These are the heart of the *Inferno* and they contain some of the most dramatic scenes, both in content and in poetic richness. The opening of this canto, with a long descriptive passage, is some of Dante's best poetry.

The first sinners that Dante confronts in the first ditch of Malebolge are the Panderers (those who used others to serve their own purposes). Due to the nature of retribution, Panderers will spend eternity prodded by malicious demons. The souls walking in the other direction are Seducers who are similar to the Panderers, because they also used others for their own needs.

Venedico Caccianemico of Bologna admits to Dante that he brought Ghisolabella, his own sister, around to suit the sexual desires of the Marquis Obbizo da Este of Ferrara. One of the demons prodding the damned soul calls Venedico a pimp.

The figure of Jason is startling in this canto, because he is quite deep in the bowels of Hell, and he is a famous mythological figure. Dante, as the poet of courtly love, clearly dislikes Jason's behavior toward women—seduce them, get them with child, and desert them.

The souls in the next ditch are the Flatterers, and again, in the theme of retribution, they wallow in filth and sewage, much like they did in life, with their false flattery. To illustrate the grossness of false flattery, Dante picks two sinners. The first, Alessio Interminelli da Lucca, was from a noble family, though not much is known about him. The second, Thaïs, is said to have received the gift of a slave from her lover, and when asked if she thanked him much, she replied with so much flattery that her gratitude was beyond believing.

Glossary

the year of the Jubilee   1300.

'sipa'   Bolognese dialect for 'yes.'

Jason   *Greek Mythology.* a prince who leads the Argonauts, and with Medea's help, gets the Golden Fleece.

Colchian Ram   the Golden Fleece.

Lemnos   Greek island in the North Aegean Sea.

Venus' curse   made the women of Lemnos smell bad so that their men would not come near them; the women eventually killed their men for refusing to come near them.

Hypsipyle   daughter of the king of Lemnos; seduced and deserted by Jason; saved her father when all the men of Lemnos were being killed.

Medea   *Greek Mythology.* a sorceress who helps Jason get the Golden Fleece and, later, when deserted by him, kills their children and his new lover.

Canto XIX

Summary

Dante and Virgil are on the rim of the third pit, ditch, or trench of Circle VIII for those guilty of Simony. These sinners used their positions in the church for personal monetary gain. The Simonists are upside-down in round holes the size of baptismal fonts.

From each of these holes protrude the feet and legs of a spirit, with the rest of the body upside down in the hole. The soles of their feet are on fire, and Dante sees one shade who is apparently suffering more torment than others, moving and shaking violently; his feet are burning more fiercely than the others.

The soul mistakes Dante for Boniface and is surprised that he is there earlier than expected. Dante tells the soul that he is mistaken, and the soul tells his story. The soul wore "the Great Mantle" of the office of the pope. Below him, in cracks in the rock, are other popes who committed the same sin. When the next pope, Boniface, joins them, he, Nicholas III, will be pushed further down into the stone. The soul says that a new and worse soul will be sent in time to cover him in the hole. Dante reproaches the spirit vehemently. Virgil is pleased at Dante's behavior and carries him out of the chasm where he looks down into the next moat.

Commentary

Theme

The two themes of religion and divine retribution collide in this chasm where the Simonists reside. Simonists, named after Simon the Magus, are souls who sold ecclesiastic favors and offices for their own personal wealth.

These sinners, the Simonists, are upside-down in holes resembling baptismal fonts, illustrating that their sin debased their office, and their feet are on fire, most likely lit by the oil of the last rites. Their time in the font is limited, however. When a new sinner comes, he takes the previous sinner's place, and the previous sinner is shoved down into the rock for eternity, much like the succession of Simonists in office.

These sinners are punished in a manner that is a curious reversal of baptismal practices of the time: Even the burning feet are from the oil used in baptism instead of the cool sweetness of the holy water.

Dante clearly finds these sinners despicable enough to pause in the narrative for a moment and rebuke them harshly. This act does not happen often in *Inferno*, and it is significant because it illustrates Dante's abhorrence of the corruption of the church that he held so dear. Dante also takes a moment out of the narrative to answer the charge of sacrilege from a number of years earlier when he saved a boy from drowning in a baptismal font by smashing it.

The sinner that Dante addresses is Pope Nicholas III, the chief sinner in the pit, demonstrated by the height of the flames on his feet. His family name meant "the bear cubs" in Italian, and he wore "the Great Mantle" of the papacy. He was a corrupt pope, according to Dante, and he awaits an even more corrupt pope, Boniface, who died in 1303. (Remember, the poem takes place in 1300, though Dante wrote it later.) After Boniface will come Boniface Clement V, an even more corrupt pope.

Throughout *Inferno*, Dante learns to rebuke and despise sin. In this canto, he feels absolutely no pity for this sinner, as he did with many sinners at the beginning of his journey, and in fact, damns him further. Virgil, as a spiritual guide and symbol for wisdom, is very pleased with Dante's actions. Dante grows more and more ready for the next legs of his journey—Purgatory and Paradise. He must purge himself of sin before he enters those places. Dante's sin is why he was turned away from the Mount of Joy in the opening canto; he must experience Hell and its dangers before he can experience the opposite.

Glossary

Simonists   persons involved in the buying or selling of sacred or spiritual things, as sacraments or benefices.

Simon Magus   a magician from whom the word "simony" is derived; tried to buy the rights and power to administer the Holy Ghost.

San Giovianni   church that Dante attended.

Jason of the Maccabees   bought an office as High Priest of the Jews.

Charles of Anjou   seventh son of Louis VIII of France.

Constantine   Constantine I (*Flavius Valerius Aurelius Constantinus*) *c.* 280–337 A.D.; emperor of Rome (306–337); converted to Christianity; called *the Great*.

Canto XX

Summary

Dante looks down upon the faces of the sinners in the next chasm and weeps with grief at their torment; these sinners must walk through eternity with their heads on backwards and tears in their eyes. Virgil reproaches Dante for feeling any pity for these sinners, the Fortune Tellers and Diviners, because they are here as a point of justice. They sinned by trying to foretell the future, which is known only to God.

As Virgil mentions Manto, one of the sinners in this chasm, he also delivers a lengthy, detailed description of how his native city, Mantua, originated, and Virgil makes Dante promise to tell this true story, should he ever have the occasion, and not let any other falsehood confuse this truth. Dante promises and asks about the others in the chasm. Virgil names a few of the souls before saying that he and Dante should hurry onward because the moon is already setting. With that, the poets travel on to the next chasm.

Commentary

Dante takes a step backward in his learning process in this canto. For the first time in Malebolge, Dante feels pity for the sinners in this circle, and Virgil chastises him for his behavior. Perhaps Dante wasn't ready to see the true nature of sin in those earlier cantos. Also possible is that Virgil is fallible and can also feel pity for some of the souls in Hell, but not for those in the final circles.

In keeping with Dante's theme of Divine Retribution, the Fortune Tellers and Diviners have their heads on backwards and their eyes are full of tears. These are the souls who, on Earth, tried to see too far ahead of them, and thus will spend eternity forever looking behind with blurred vision. Following the teachings of the papacy, the theme of religion is broached, because the papacy did not approve of sorcery in any form.

Dante the Poet tries to negate Virgil's reputation as a white magician here, a sin that would certainly place him in this chasm with the Fortune Tellers and Diviners. By alleviating Virgil of the guilt-by-association of being born in a city founded by a sorceress, Dante hopes to show that Virgil is innocent of sorcery. Virgil explains, in his long tangent about Mantua, that the land was initially inhabited by Manto, but that men came, and with no further magic, founded the city and named it after her. It is important that Dante's guide not be associated with such things that would taint his journey.

For the first time, Dante violates his own concept of judging each spirit by the standards of the time in which he lived. Here he condemns the Greek prophets, who were held in high esteem in their own time. It is interesting that the Old Testament prophets are not here, and Dante offers no explanation for their absence.

Glossary

Thebans   citizens of Thebes, the chief city of ancient Greece.

Amphiareus   one of the seven captains who fought against Thebes.

Tiresias   *Greek Mythology.* a blind soothsayer of Thebes.

Aruns   a soothsayer from Etruria.

Luni   an ancient Etruscan city.

Manto   sorceress after whom Mantua is named.

Bacchus   *Greek and Roman Mythology.* the god of wine and revelry.

Tyrolean   of Tyrol.

Garda   lake in Northern Italy, on the Lombardy-Veneto border.

Po   river in Northern Italy, flowing from the Cottian Alps east into the Adriatic.

Mantua   commune in Lombardy, Northern Italy; birthplace of Virgil.

Eurypylus   Greek augur.

Michael Scot   Irish scholar; dealt with the occult.

Guido Bonatti   court astrologer and military adviser.

Cain with his bush of thorns   the moon.

Cantos XXI and XXII

Summary

In Canto XXI, Dante and Virgil make their way to the fifth chasm, which is very dark and filled with boiling pitch. Dante compares the pitch to the material used to caulk the seams of ships. Suddenly, a raging demon appears, and Virgil hides Dante behind a large rock so he can go to the demons and make a deal for their safe passage.

The demon is carrying a sinner, which he tosses into the pitch, saying that he is going back for more sinners to place in the chasm of Grafters. The other demons warn the sinner to get beneath the pitch or the sinners will taste their grappling hooks.

Virgil confronts the demons, and they threaten to harm him. He asks to speak to one of them, and Malacoda, leader of the demons, steps forward. After hearing about Virgil's divinely inspired journey, Malacoda grants the poets safe passage and rounds up a group of ten demons to escort them to the next bridge. The poets must travel on the next bridge, because as Malacoda tells them, the closest bridge fell in an earthquake 1,266 years, one day, and five hours from the present point in time (indicating the Harrowing of Hell on the day that Christ died).

Dante is afraid of the demons and pleads with Virgil to go on without them, but Virgil reprimands him for his fear and reminds him that the demons are there only to guard and torture the sinners in the stew of pitch. After a vulgar sign and countersign between the demons, the poets move on with their escorts.

In Canto XXII, Dante marvels that he is in such terrible company, but he realizes that this part of his trek with the demons is necessary. Every now and then a sinner shows his back at the surface of the pitch to ease his pain, and Dante compares them to frogs squatting about in water with only their muzzles sticking out.

One sinner is slow in ducking back into the pitch fast enough and is caught by one of the demons who pulls him out of the pitch by his hair. Before the demons tear him to shreds, Dante asks if he can listen to the sinner's history. The sinner replies that he was born in Navarre and worked for a king and began to graft, which is the reason he now suffers in the pitch. The demons begin to tear at the sinner, and to avoid this punishment, he offers them a deal. The sinner says that he will whistle, as if he'd been set free, and call more sinners (especially Italians with whom Dante will want to speak) to the surface of the pitch, so that they can suffer at the hands of the demons as well.

The demons are suspicious, but they let him try his plan, warning him that if he tried to escape they would catch him. The sinner, once set free, jumps off of the ridge into the safety of the pitch and escapes. The demons, furious at the deception, fly after him. When they see that he has escaped, two of the demons begin fighting, fall into the pitch, and are unable to rise. The other demons form a rescue party and while they are occupied, the poets use the opportunity to slip away unnoticed.

Commentary

Style & Language

The language and imagery in Cantos XXI and XXII is coarse and full of grotesque imagery, far more than earlier cantos, suggesting that the lower a person travels in Hell, the more grotesque Hell becomes. The demons in these cantos are described as no other beasts in the *Inferno* are described, with great detail and an almost comic-relief like quality. Dante the Pilgrim is simultaneously afraid of and fascinated by these beasts.

Theme

Like the rest of the sinners in Hell, the Grafters also experience Dante's concept of Divine Retribution. Because they had "sticky" hands in life, stealing and embezzling money, they are damned to spend eternity in sticky pitch, and, just as their dealings were hidden from the world in life, their souls are hidden beneath the pitch in death. On Earth, Grafters took every opportunity to take advantage of others, and they are now overseen by terrible demons that use every opportunity to take advantage of them.

Character Insight

Virgil's behavior changes in these deeper circles. No longer does he coddle and behave tenderly toward Dante. In fact, he rebukes Dante twice in Canto XXI, once for hiding behind the rocks (where Virgil placed him) and once for being afraid of the demons. Dante seems almost reluctant to continue the journey, literally and spiritually, and Virgil, as human reason, is frustrated with him.

All that is known about the Grafter from Navarre is what he says of himself. He, as the other sinners in Hell, is unchanged and shows no remorse for his sins; as he was in life, so he remains in Hell. The scene of this sinner and his escape from the demons functions to allow the poets to progress on their journey; there is no other real reason for its presence in the narrative.

Glossary

Santa Zita   the Patron Saint of Lucca.

Bonturo   politician of Lucca.

Serchio   a river near Lucca.

Pisan   a person from the city of Pisa of Pisa.

Caprona   a fortress near Pisa.

Sardinia   Italian island in the Mediterranean, south of Corsica; or the region of Italy comprising this island and small nearby islands.

Canto XXIII

Summary

The poets walk unattended for a while, and Dante muses on Aesop's fable of the mouse and the frog. Then they arrive at the next chasm which is filled with spirits walking very slowly, as with a heavy burden.

These shades are the Hypocrites. They wear cloaks and hoods that are dazzling with their glitter but lined with lead. Dante and Virgil turn to the left, but they are walking faster than the weighted-down Hypocrites, so Dante asks Virgil to slow down and find a spirit that he might know.

A spirit calls to Dante, recognizing his Tuscan speech, and asks him to wait. Two spirits approach without speaking. Finally, one observes that Dante must be alive because his throat moves. Speaking to Dante, they ask why he has come to this valley of Hypocrites and who he is.

Dante tells them he is a Florentine and is indeed alive; in turn, he asks who they are who weep so bitterly and what their punishment is. They answer that they were of the order of the Jovial Friars and had been named to govern Florence jointly, in order to keep peace.

Dante angrily begins to speak to the friars of their evil, when he sees a figure on the ground held by three stakes. Friar Catalan explains that this is Caiaphas, the high priest who told the council of Pharisees that it was better for Jesus to die than for the whole nation to perish. Therefore, he lies where each one who passes by must step upon him, and his father-in-law (Annas) and the Council are punished in the same manner. Virgil looks at Caiaphas for some time.

Finally, he turns and asks the friar if there is a bridge over the chasm. The friar answers that all were destroyed at the same time, but the travelers may climb out of the ruins of the one nearby, without much difficulty.

Commentary

This canto deals with the Hypocrites, represented by Caiaphas. For their punishment, they are forced to wear coats that are beautiful on the outside, but lined inside with heavy lead, forcing them to bend over and struggle to move. This punishment fits the sin since they glitter on the outside but are so weighted down that there is no chance of spiritual progress.

Dante uses the fable of the mouse and the frog (then attributed to Aesop) as an allegory to describe the scene in Cantos XXII between the demons and the escaped sinner. The fable goes that a mouse wanted to cross a pond and asked a frog to help him. The frog, wanting to drown the mouse, suggested that he take the mouse across on his back. The mouse agreed, but was afraid of falling off, so the frog suggested that the mouse tie himself to the frog. When they reach the middle of the pond, the frog decides to dive under and pull the mouse with him. However, a hawk, seeing the struggling mouse, catches it, taking the frog with him. In Dante's comparison, the sinner represents the mouse and the demons that fell into the pitch represent the frog. There are several disagreements about which creature represents what.

Virgil, the ever-diligent guide, returns to his tender nature when possible harm may come to Dante. He lifts Dante like a son and bears him safely to the bottom of the sixth pit. Dante is relieved at this action, which again confirms Virgil's fitness as a guide.

Dante's two themes of religion and politics collide again in the sixth pit. The Jovial Friars were an order founded to keep peace and enforce order. Of the two friars that Dante encounters here, one was a Guelph and one was a Ghibelline. Both friars were jointly appointed to help bring peace to Florence. However, their reign resulted in much bloodshed and violence, and they were shortly removed from office.

Because the chasm of the Hypocrites is chiefly filled with sinners with whom religion played a major role in their damnation, it is fitting that Caiaphas, High Priest of the Jews, is the chief sinner of the pit, having been crucified to the ground to suffer being walked upon for all eternity. Caiaphas advised Pontius Pilate to condemn Jesus to death on the cross for the supposed benefit of the city. Virgil marvels at his appearance because he was not yet there when Virgil made his first trip to the depths of Hell.

In the circle of the Hypocrites, Dante is again recognized as being alive, this time because his throat moves as he talks. The cloaks of the Hypocrites, which dazzle the eye, actually are instruments of torture. Moreover, the heavy garments they wear force the sinners to adopt a decorous and subdued attitude which is entirely in character with their worldly habit of hiding a vicious nature beneath a virtuous and holy appearance.

Dante has placed the Hypocrites far down in the circles of Hell. Their presence is a restatement of Dante's definition of sin as perversion of the intellect. Few sins can equal the deliberate cloaking of one's true character and feelings in a false aspect of piety, tolerance or honesty.

Glossary

Aesop   real or legendary Greek author of fables; supposed to have lived in the sixth century B.C.

Frederick's capes   Frederick II executed people by placing them in a leaden shell which was then melted around them.

Jovial Friars   the nickname of the monks of the Glorious Virgin Mary from Bolongna.

Bolognese   of Bologna, its people, or their dialect.

Pharisees   a member of an ancient Jewish party or fellowship that carefully observed the written law but also accepted the oral (or traditional) law; advocated democratization of religious practices; mainly they hated Jesus for questioning their authority.

Cantos XXIV and XXV

Summary

Virgil's anger, even though it is not directed at him, has made Dante as downcast and as troubled as a shepherd without a pasture for his sheep. Dante is dependent upon his master not only for physical help, but also for spiritual guidance and moral support, and it now seems to Dante that this has been withdrawn. But one look from Virgil soon calms his spirit because Virgil is now the same serene person as he was at their first meeting.

The climb to the next bridge presents problems. Virgil is weightless, but he has to give very careful directions for Dante to test each rock before he puts his weight on it.

They both climb to the top of the sixth chasm, but Dante is out of breath. They walk to the end of the bridge, where it rests on the wall between the seventh and eighth chasms, and look down on the mass of strange serpents below them.

After the poets reach the end of the bridge, they can see the masses of serpents and sinners in the seventh chasm where the Thieves reside. The sinners are naked, and their hands are tied behind them with a serpent whose head and tail are threaded through the spirit's body at the loins and tied in coils and knots at the front. Another serpent sinks its fangs in the neck of a shade, who immediately takes afire, burns to ashes, and falls on the ground, only to resume its shape and its torment once again. This shade seems as bewildered by what has happened as one who has been the victim of a seizure of some kind.

Dante asks the shade who he is, and he answers that he came recently from Tuscany, where he lived the life of a beast. He is Vanni Fucci of Pistoia. Dante asks what his crime was, for he had seen him once and considered him to be a man of violence. The spirit, ashamed, confesses that it hurts him more for Dante to see him here in this dreadful place than it did to be condemned to this chasm of thieves. In obscure language, he prophesizes that Dante's party shall suffer greatly.

Canto XXV opens with the same sinner, Fucci, making "figs" with his hands and blaspheming God. A Centaur, Cacus, races up to the group and asks the location of the blasphemer. Virgil explains to Dante that Cacus does not reside with his fellows at the banks of Phlegethon because he stole Hercules' cattle. Hercules avenged the theft by clubbing Cacus to death, and he continued clubbing long after Cacus was dead. Suddenly, hoards of serpents climb on to Fucci and a dragon perches on his shoulders.

The Centaur leaves and three sinners appear, apparently concerned, asking if a sinner named Cianfa has fallen back. At that moment a six-legged lizard fastens itself to one of the three sinners, Agnello, and weaves itself through the sinner's body, melding it with the sinner, like hot wax. The two beasts become one and the other two sinners mock Agnello.

A small black monster runs up to one of the remaining two sinners and bites him near his bellybutton. A mutual transformation begins. The monster takes on the human form of the sinner, and the sinner takes on the monster's form.

Commentary

Theme

In keeping with Dante's theme of retribution, where the punishment fits the sin, the Thieves in the seventh chasm consistently steal one another's forms, and they are condemned to spend eternity with their hands bound. Just as they stole the substance of others in life, they have their only substance (their body forms) stolen throughout their eternal damnation in death.

Character Insight

Dante becomes afraid when Virgil shows signs of confusion and weakness. Dante relies on Virgil, who symbolizes human reason and wisdom, to deliver him from Hell, and when his guide shows signs of failure, he becomes irritated and fearful. Virgil was deceived by Malacoda and, as a result, is off track. Virgil's confusion illustrates the fallibility of human wisdom. Dante uses this fallibility to illustrate his notion that only things that are divine can reach perfection, and even though Virgil is a great guide, he cannot ever reach perfection. Dante shows his all-too-human side at the opening of Canto XXIV, where he can barely climb from the chasm of the Hypocrites. He does not belong in Hell, and he is tiring physically from this journey; fortunately, it is almost at a close.

Dante again uses prophecy as a devise to further the political narrative of his poem. The main action in the seventh chasm begins with Vanni Fucci, who was a Black Guelph in Piceno and was accused of stealing from the sacristy. His presence in this pit is not as significant as his malicious prophecy against Dante, who was a White Guelph. His prophecy is that there will be a battle at Pistoia and that the battle will result in wounding the Whites. Indeed, this did happen in 1302, far before Dante wrote this part of *Inferno*.

The main action of Canto XXV, besides the serpents swarming Fucci and obscuring him, is the action surrounding the Five Thieves of Florence. Little is known specifically about them beyond the fact that they were thieves, but Dante apparently knew of their reputations. These thieves are damned to spend eternity stealing one another's forms.

The transformation of the spirits and the serpents are described at length with terrifying vividness. Watching in horrified fascination, Dante seems to be recalling an evil nightmare, and words fail him at the end—an effective literary device that he will use again.

Glossary

chelidrids, jaculi, phareans, cenchriads, amphisbands various reptilian creatures that torture the sinners in the seventh pit.

Ethiopia ancient kingdom (possibly dating to the tenth century B.C.) in Northeastern Africa, on the Red Sea, corresponding to modern Sudan and Northern Ethiopia (the country).

Red Sea sea between Northeastern Africa and Western Arabia; connected with the Mediterranean Sea by the Suez Canal and with the Indian Ocean by the Gulf of Aden.

Black Black Guelph.

White White Guelph.

making figs an obscene gesture, still used in Italy today.

Maremma low, unhealthful, but fertile marshy land near the sea, especially in Italy.

Gaville refering to Francesco dei Cavalcanti, who was killed by the people of Gaville; many townspeople were then killed by his kinsmen avenging his death.

Cantos **XXVI** and **XXVII**

Summary

Canto XXVI opens with a passionate address to Dante's native Florence, saying that there are so many Florentines populating Hell because of the terrible actions of its citizens. Dante prophesizes that a day of mourning will come to Florence, and not a day too soon.

The poets move on to the eighth chasm where Dante sees thousands of little flames, reminding him of fireflies on a hillside. He leans so far forward on the ledge of the bridge that he almost falls into the chasm. Virgil says that each of the flames contains a sinner, which is hidden from view by the fire surrounding it. These are the Evil Counselors, people that used their power and their intellect for evil. Dante remarks that he already figured out that each flame contained a sinner, and that he wishes to speak with a great flame that splits away into two horns of fire. This two-pronged flame conceals Ulysses and Diomede, who are in Hell because of three evil deeds: the ambush of the Trojan Horse; the weeping of Deidamia, the King's daughter whom Achilles abandoned; and the matter of the theft of Pallas Athena's statue at the Palladium. Because Dante is Italian, Virgil suggests that he speak with them instead, because they are Greek and may scorn Dante's manner of speaking.

Virgil speaks to the flame and Ulysses, who makes up the larger part of the flame, begins to tell the story of his death. He had wanderlust and convinced a few of his friends to take a long journey with him. They sailed for five months beyond Hercules' Pillars and came to a giant mountain. As they sailed towards it, a storm broke and sunk the ship.

At the opening of Canto XXVII, Virgil allows the flame of Ulysses and Diomede to depart, and he turns his attention to another flame that wishes to tell his tale. This flame contains the soul of Count Guido da Montefeltro, who wants to know news from the upper world about his native city, Romagna. Dante tells him that Romagna is never without war and goes on to give him details of the recent past.

Dante wishes to know this shade's name, and mistaking Dante for a spirit as well, the shade answers with a bit of his history. He was a man of arms who hoped to make amends for his connection with arms by joining the Franciscans and becoming a friar. The "Great Priest" (Pope Boniface VIII), however, asked him for counsel about how to destroy his enemies. Thus, the shade was thrust back into his old sins. After he died, St. Francis came to retrieve him, but a devil said that this shade's name was written in his book because the shade resolved to give false counsel.

After hearing the spirit's story, the poets move to the ninth pit, where the Sowers of Discord reside.

Commentary

At the beginning of Canto XXVI, Dante uses another political prophecy to propel the narrative and his political theme forward. Dante actually wishes this dark prophecy on his city. Because Dante was exiled at the time he wrote *Inferno*, these events had already come to pass.

The retribution that the sinners of the eighth chasm suffer fits with the sin that they perpetrated in life. They gave evil counsel (particularly to religious leaders), and therefore, misused God's gifts. These souls worked in hidden ways, and they will spend eternity hidden from sight and burning in flames that symbolize a guilty conscience.

The most dramatic event in Canto XXVI is Dante's meeting with Ulysses. Note that Ulysses and Diomede are punished for events that would have been acceptable, even praised, in the time in which they lived. Dante again falters from his concept that sinners are only punished according to the social standards of their time. Ulysses carried out the strategy of the Trojan Horse, which led to the fall of Troy and, eventually, to the founding of the Roman line by Aeneas. Because Dante is partial to the Roman Empire, he sees this act as evil; however, another poet may see it as virtuous. Ulysses is also in the pit for two other acts: convincing Achilles to go on a journey, which caused Deidamia to die of heartbreak, and stealing a statue of Pallas from the Palladium, thus ensuring the downfall of Troy.

Virgil telling Dante not to speak to Ulysses and Diomede is significant, because the two shades would perceive Dante as a descendant of Aeneas (because he spoke Italian) and associate him with the fallen Trojans. Virgil, on the other hand, is a virtuous poet who sang their praises and is thus better suited to speak with them. Also, Dante does not speak Greek. But, Dante does not provide an explanation for how he understands Ulysses.

Dante returns to his religious theme with the soul that the poets address in Canto XXVII, that of Count Guido da Montefeltro, a fallen friar who gave evil counsel to Pope Boniface. Dante does not miss an opportunity to bring attention to his belief that Boniface is evil; his name is scattered over the whole of *Inferno*, though he is not there presently—he was still alive in 1300.

There is a great deal of symbolism and metaphor in Cantos XXVI and XXVII, perhaps more than anywhere else in *Inferno*. The language deserves mention: Dante, at this point in the narrative, becomes a better and tighter poet, able to speak in distinctive voices that seem genuine. For example, compare the power of the voice of Ulysses to some of the other stories in the text. Dante's narration of Ulysses' last voyage is some of the best poetry and one of the highlights of the entire *Inferno*.

The story is apparently an invention by Dante, and while beautiful in itself, serves also to display Dante's increasing sureness of touch in the handling of his material. Ulysses seems to be speaking in his own words, not Dante's, in contrast with the story of Francesca. The story of Ulysses is the compelling, unembellished yarn of an experienced and courageous sailor.

Glossary

Prato Cardianal Niccolo da Prato.

Eteocles *Greek Mythology.* a son of Oedipus and Jocasta.

Polynices *Greek Mythology.* a son of Oedipus and Jocasta.

Ulysses the hero of Homer's *Odyssey*; a king of Ithaca and one of the Greek leaders in the Trojan War.

Diomede *Greek Legend.* a Greek warrior at the siege of Troy who helps Ulysses steal the statue of Athena.

ambush of the Horse the Trojan Horse.

Circe in Homer's *Odyssey*, an enchantress who turns men into swine.

Penelope Ulysses' wife who waits faithfully for his return from the Trojan War.

Sicillian bull an instrument of torture in which a person is placed inside a brass bull that is then placed over a fire; holes cut in the bull emit the tortured's cries, sounding like a bull.

Verrucchio   the castle of Malatesta.

Great Priest   Pope Boniface III.

Prince of the New Pharisees   Pope Boniface III.

Silvestro   Pope who took refuge from Constantine during the persecutions of the Christians; later, he is said to have cured Constantine of leprosy.

Canto XXVIII

Summary

The canto opens with Dante wondering how to describe the sinners in the ninth chasm. This is the place of the Sowers of Discord and Scandal, and the Creators of Schism within the papacy. He warns that the punishment in this part of Hell is bloody and grotesque. Indeed, the sinners in the ninth chasm are damned to walk around the chasm until they arrive at a devil who slashes them with a long sword, according to the nature of their sin.

The first one Dante sees is Mahomet, disemboweled, who tells him that his son-in-law, Ali, is in the same condition and that all the others are horribly mangled in some manner. As they circle the chasm, the wounds heal, but when they complete the circle, the wounds are renewed by a devil with a sword.

Mahomet explains that these sinners were responsible for scandal and rift, and therefore, they are torn apart as they tore others apart in life. Mahomet asks Dante to tell Fra Dolcino, who is still alive, to store food for the winter or risk joining him in the chasm. After asking Dante to warn his friend, Mahomet moves on.

Another soul addresses Dante and asks that he warn Guido and Angiolello that they will be thrown from their ships into the sea by the one-eyed traitor (Malatestino). Dante will bear this sinner's name to the upper world, if he shows him a soul he spoke of as having seen the land of the traitor.

Although the soul is standing right beside Dante, he cannot speak because his tongue is chopped out. This soul is Curio, by whose council Caesar crossed the Rubicon, thus starting a war.

A third shade, Mosca dei Lamberti, calls out that he too wishes to be remembered, but Dante wishes death to all his kindred, and he runs off like a madman.

A headless figure approaches Dante, holding his head in front of him as if it were a lantern. The figure holds his head up to the poets, so they can hear him better. The figure says that he is Bertrand de Born, and that he set the young king to mutiny against his own father. Born also states that, because he parted father and son, he spends eternity with his head parted from his body.

Commentary

In keeping with the theme of Divine Retribution that runs throughout *Inferno*, the sinners in the ninth chasm, the Sowers of Discord, are brutally split and mutilated, just as they split and mutilated aspects of religion, politics, or kinsmen. Each sinner is punished according to degree of sin, as well as suffering punishment specifically geared toward their particular sin. For example, Curio's tongue is cut out because his sin was false advice, and Bertrand de Born has his head cut off because he caused a rift between father and son.

Dante obviously sees Mahomet as one of the chief sinners responsible for the division between Christianity and Islam. Dante blames Mahomet's successor, Ali, as well. Dante describes these two shades as being split in two, just as he feels they split the church. The next three sinners sowed political discord and are punished appropriately, especially Mosca, who has both of his arms hacked off. Mosca advised the death of a man who had broken an engagement (which was a good as a marriage vow in Dante's time). The death of the man resulted in the beginning of a long feud between the Guelphs and the Ghibellines of Florence, tearing the city asunder. This feud ultimately resulted in a great political schism that resulted in Dante's exile, so it is no wonder that Dante treats this spirit so brutally. Finally, Bertrand de Born, the man whose head was removed, caused a rift between family members.

Ironically, Dante is less brutal and grotesque in his language when describing Bertrand de Born, even though he is in the last category of sinners, closest to the center of Hell. Dante spares the gore that he uses to describe the previous sinners, especially that of Mahomet.

Glossary

Livy (Latin name *Titus Livius*)   59 B.C.–17 A.D.; Roman historian.

Mahomet   *c.* 570–632 A.D.; Arab prophet; founder of Islam.

Ali   *c.* 600–661 A.D.; fourth caliph of Islam (656–661), considered the first caliph by the Shiites; son-in-law of Mahomet.

Neptune *Roman Mythology*. the god of the sea; the same as the Greek Poseidon.

Cyprus country on an island at the east end of the Mediterranean, south of Turkey.

Majorca island of Spain, largest of the Balearic Islands.

Argive of ancient Argos or Argolis.

Rubicon small river in northern Italy that formed the boundary between Cisalpine Gaul and the Roman Republic; when Caesar crossed it (49 B.C.) at the head of his army to march on Rome, he began the civil war with Pompey.

Absalom *Bible*. David's favorite son; killed after rebelling against his father: 2 Samuel 18.

David *Bible*. the second king of Israel and Judah, succeeding Saul; reputed to be the writer of many psalms.

Cantos XXIX and XXX

Summary

Having arrived at the chasm or evil pouch in the eighth circle, Dante wants to stop for a moment to observe these suffering shades, but Virgil is impatient and tells him to move along. Dante tells Virgil that he is seeking one of his own kinsmen who, he believes, is here. "I think a spirit of my own blood is among the dammed." Dante is tarrying only because he wants to speak with this relative, and he wishes Virgil would be more patient.

Virgil responds that he saw Dante's kinsman under the bridge that they had just crossed, and that this shade, which the others had called Geri del Bello, had shaken its finger threateningly at Dante as they passed by. It is then that Dante realizes that the murder of Geri del Bello had never been revenged by any member of Dante's family. And for this failure, Dante expresses his sorrow for his un-avenged kinsman.

While Virgil and Dante are talking, they reach the bridge over the tenth and final chasm of the eighth circle. Here they see the suffering and hear the wails and weeping of the Falsifiers. The noise is so loud that Dante covers his ears, and the stench is so powerful that it reminds him of rotting human flesh, lying exposed to the world.

Dante compares their state to that of the miserable people who cram the hospitals at three different cities. These souls lay about, as if dying from pestilence and disease. Some lay gasping, some lean on one another, and some pick one another's scabs as if scaling a fish.

Virgil interrupts two of the souls who are picking at each other's scabs and asks them if there are any Italians (Latians) among them. One replies that they are Italian and once Virgil explains their presence in the circle, the souls tell their history. One is from Arezzo and he supposedly joked with Albert of Siena that he could fly and thus, he was burned for the lie, though he is in this circle for alchemy, another form of falsifying. The other soul is Capocchio, Dante's friend in his school days, who was burned for alchemy in 1293.

Dante begins Canto XXX with a long metaphorical mythological comparison to describe the rage of the two spirits that come furiously out of the darkness, one of which descends on Capocchio. The other alchemist tells Dante that this raging beast was Gianni Schicchi, who impersonated a dead man so that he cold benefit from the will. The other raging shade is Myrrha, who posed as another and mated with her father; once caught, she changed herself into a tree and bore Adonis from the trunk. These are the Evil Impersonators, damned to rage though Hell and seize on souls, and in turn, they are seized upon by one another.

The next class of Falsifiers that the poets encounter is in the form of Master Adam, a Counterfeiter who made florins from alloyed gold and was burned for the offense. On top of his afflictions and the curse of not being able to move, he is damned with extreme thirst, though his belly is waterlogged. He says that he imagines sweet water running from the Arno's banks.

Finally, the poets meet a soul of the final class of Falsifiers, Sinon the Greek, a False Witness who beguiled the citizens of Troy to allow the Trojan Horse into the gate of Troy, thus allowing the soldiers inside to wreak havoc on that city. And they also meet Potiphar, who falsely accused Joseph.

Master Adam and Sinon the Greek exchange blows and begin bickering about who is the worse sinner. Sinon says that he is there for one sin, while Master Adam is there for thousands—each coin being a separate sin. Dante listens, fascinated, until Virgil reproaches him soundly, and Dante is overcome with shame, so much so that he cannot speak. Virgil senses his shame and says that less shame would wash away a greater fault, but that to listen to such petty arguing is degrading.

Commentary

In Dante's time there was a tradition, even a right protected by law, of avenging the death of kinsman. Geri del Bello's death had not been avenged at the time of the writing of the *Inferno*, though the death was avenged thirty years later by del Bello's nephews with the accepted code of "a life for a life."

Virgil upbraids Dante for weeping and pausing at the ninth pit, consistent with the hardening of his character in these later circles. There is no time for pure emotion at this point in the journey; time is growing short and Virgil must move Dante along, even if that means taking on a harsher nature. Dante is still utterly human, his emotions changing with each moment of the journey, though he is coming to realize that his pity does not change the fate of these sinners, that his only proactive choices are to remember them to the upper world, and in some cases, cause a sinner more pain.

The final chasm of Circle VII contains the Falsifiers, who are, as are the other sinners in other circles, suffering the pain of retribution. These sinners affected the senses of others, showing themselves or substances to be what they are not, thus they spend eternity in a corruption of the senses—filth, thirst, disease, stench, darkness, horrible shrieking, physical pain—these sinners are damned to an eternity of what they put others through in life. In Canto XXX, the two mythological examples of insanity are a link and/or a parallel the two sinners in this circle who suffer from insanity.

As usual, Dante gives faces to each of these four classes of sins, in allowing the sinners to speak. It is noteworthy what sins Dante considers worse than others. Here, there are four classes of falsification, ranging from those that harm others least to those that harm others most. This is in keeping with Dante's positioning of all of the sinners in Hell—those on the inside of any given chasm were less outwardly harmful than the others that are closer to the center of Hell.

Interestingly, the sinners here that are allowed to tell their tale are only vaguely related to religion or politics, though one could argue that they are connected to both in some manner. Remember, Virgil stated earlier that God despised Malice the most, out of all of the possible sins, and these souls in the final chasm of Circle VII are certainly guilty of Malice—they knew exactly what they were doing, and they did it with malicious intent.

In this particular canto, readers should note that the sinners aren't suffering from an outside, foreign influence in the environment as in the other cantos. The sinners here are suffering from systemic infection within themselves. Alchemists have leprosy, impersonators are mad, counterfeiters have dropsy, and the liars have a fever that makes them stink. They are punished by the corrupt state of their minds and bodies. Their corrupt sense of values is symbolized by the corrupt state of their minds and bodies.

Character Insight

Just before the poets leave this circle, Virgil gives Dante a strict and swift reprimand, again illustrating how he has changed from the earlier circles. Dante is immediately filled with shame, something that probably would not have happened in an earlier circle, where he would not have known better than to listen to two shades bickering. Dante is coming to understand the nature of sin and is learning to be disgusted by it. Virgil sees his immediate shame and is relieved at this behavior; Virgil's toughness on Dante is teaching him to be diligent and watchful, though Virgil indicates that something similar may happen again, illustrating that he understands the fallibility of Human Nature.

Glossary

Daedalus   *Greek Mythology.* the skillful artist and builder of the Labyrinth in Crete, from which, by means of wings he made, he and his son Icarus escaped.

Alchemy   an early form of chemistry, with magical associations. Its chief aims were to change base metals into gold and to discover the elixir of perpetual youth.

Juno   *Roman Mythhology.* the sister and wife of Jupiter, queen of the gods, and goddess of marriage.

Semele   daughter of King Cadmus of Thebes.

King Athamas   Semele's brother-in-law.

Hecuba   taken to Greece from Troy as a slave; written about by Ovid.

Baptist's image   John the Baptist's image was stamped on gold florins.

Guido, Alessandro   the Counts of Guidi.

Narcissus' mirror   *Greek Myth.* a beautiful youth who, after Echo's death, is made to pine away for love of his own reflection in a spring and changes into the narcissus.

Canto XXXI

Summary

The poets climb to the top of the stony chasm that ends the eighth circle and they begin their approach to the ninth and final circle, which is a great, dark pit filled with ice and cold, strong winds caused by Lucifer beating his wings. Dante thinks that he sees a city with many towers in the distance, but Virgil tells him that his eyes deceive him. The towers are actually the Giants, plugged into the center of the well up to their waists. Indeed, as they grow closer, Dante sees the Giants clearly, and at close range, Dante says that Nature was wise to discontinue the creation of these monsters. One of the Giants is Nimrod, builder of the tower of Babel, and he speaks in a nonsense tongue. Virgil reprimands Nimrod, calling him stupid and telling him that his horn is around his neck. Nimrod is condemned to babble through eternity, not understanding and not being understood.

The second Giant the poets encounter is Ephialtes, who endeavored with the other Giants to war against the gods. Ephialtes is bound with a chain five times around his body, and Dante wonders who could have had the strength to bind the Giant. Ephialtes begins to rock back and forth, causing the ground to tremble and scaring Dante.

The third Giant they meet is Antaeus, and Virgil praises him for his deeds and strength on Earth and, with this flattery, gains passage on Antaeus' palm down to the bottom of the pit, the final circle of Hell, Cocytus. Dante is terrified that the Giant will harm him, but Antaeus gently places the poets on the bottom of the final hole.

Commentary

Retribution is not the main concern of this canto, as it has been in previous cantos, though it is easy to see how at least two of these Giants come to be the guardians of the final circle. Nimrod, the legendary king of Babylon, constructed the Tower of Babel to reach heaven, but he was prevented from doing so by a confusion of tongues. This Giant is damned to spend eternity babbling, without any comprehension of himself or others. The second Giant, Ephialtes, son of Neptune, warred against the gods, and so has his arms bound so that he can do no more harm. The third Giant, Antaeus, is there for the many murders he committed; he should be in another circle, but suffers with the other Giants merely because of his nature as a Giant. Antaeus is the son of Neptune (the sea) and Tellus (the Earth) and was invincible, as long as he touched the Earth, his mother. Hercules killed him by holding him over his head and strangling him in mid-air. He is unchained because he did not join the other Giants against the gods. Here, again, the sinner with the worse sin is punished more harshly.

Literary Device

This canto functions largely as a device to get the poets to the final circle, Cocytus, where Satan resides, and it also serves to introduce the reader to the next division of hell. The Giants serve as another terror that Dante must encounter and can also be read as symbols for the worst that human nature has to offer—these beasts are powerful slaves to their passions. Dante even says that Nature was right when she decided to stop producing them.

The Fallen Angels guarding the gates of the City in Canto VIII are analogous to the Giants guarding Cocytus, as both the Fallen Angels and the Giants are guarding boundaries and serve to link the parts of Lower Hell together. They are also analogous because both groups rebelled against their gods, and the basis of all the sins punished in Lower Hell is Envy and Pride. This canto revolves around the pride of the Giants and also explains the extreme evil of these Giants as intellect joined with brute force and evil will.

Glossary

Jove *Roman Mythology.* the chief deity; god of thunder and the skies.

Mars *Roman Mythology.* the god of war.

Hannibal 247c.–183 B.C.; Carthaginian general; crossed the Alps to invade Italy in 218 B.C.

High Olympus mountain in Northern Greece, between Thessaly and Macedonia; *c.* 9,580 ft. (2,920 m); in Greek mythology, the home of the gods.

Judas Judas Iscariot, the disciple who betrayed Jesus: Matt. 26:14, 48.

Lucifer Satan; specifically, in Christian theology, Satan is the leader of the fallen angels. He was an angel of light until he revolted against God and, with the others, was cast into hell.

Cantos XXXII and XXXIII

Summary

Whereas earlier, Dante searched for rhymes that would help alleviate the suffering of the shades in the upper circles, now he calls out for "rhymes rugged and harsh and hoarse/ fit for the hideous hole" [Sayers' translation]—horrible words befitting the utter horror of this most horrendous place, the very bottom of Hell, reserved for the most heinous sinners.

A soul cries out for Dante to be careful not to tread on the heads of the souls in that frozen lake, and Dante turns and sees that the sinners are frozen according to their sin. Dante and Virgil are in the first of four rounds of the final circle, Cocytus. The first round is called Caina, and the sinners here have their heads bowed toward the ice, chattering their teeth and crying.

Dante looks around and sees two sinners clamped tightly together, breast-to-breast, and asks them who they are, to which they do not reply but butt their heads together like goats. A nearby sinner with his ears frozen off replies that these two were brothers, and that there are no two more deserving of punishment in all of Caina than these two. He goes on to name other sinners, and finally himself.

Moving further towards the center of Hell, Dante accidentally kicks the face of a sinner, who yells at Dante, asking him why he would want to cause him more pain. Dante asks Virgil for a moment to speak with the sinner, and his wish is granted. The sinner asks Dante who he thinks he is, kicking the faces of the sinners in Antenora, the second round of the ninth circle. Dante replies that if the shade tells him his name, he will make him famous on Earth. The shade does not want to comply, and Dante grabs a handful of the shade's hair and threatens to tear it out if he does not give his name. The shade says he does not care if Dante should rip until his brain lies bare; he will not tell, to which Dante rips out tufts of the sinner's hair. A nearby sinner tells Dante the name of the reluctant sinner, Bocca, who then will not shut up as Dante commands, telling him the names of many other sinners in the round with him.

Upon leaving Bocca, Dante comes across two sinners in such close proximity that one is feeding off of the back of the other's neck. Dante offers to tell the sinner's story in the upper world, if the sinner would tell it.

Canto XXXIII opens with the sinner's tale. He was Count Ugolino, and the soul he feeds upon was Archbishop Ruggieri, on whom he trusted. Ruggieri imprisoned Ugolino and his four sons in a tower, nailed the doors shut, and starved them all to death. Ugolino is forced to watch his young boys starve one by one. And his hatred for Ruggieri increases with each of his son's death. Once through with his long and passionate tale, Ugolino goes back to feeding on Ruggieri.

As the poets move along, they come to a place where the souls are not placed vertically in the ice, but they are supine with only their faces raised out of the ice. As a result, their tears freeze in their eyes, creating little crystal visors over their eye sockets. Dante is beginning to feel chilled and also feels a wind blowing over the ice—Virgil says that the source of the wind will soon be known.

One of the shades locked up to the face in the ice of Ptolomea, the third round of the ninth circle, begs Dante to remove the sheath of ice over his eyes so that he may cry freely for a while. Dante promises to do so if the shade tells him his name, saying that he will go to the last rim of the ice if he does not keep his promise. The shade complies, saying that he was Friar Albergio.

Dante, sure that Friar Albergio is not yet dead, is shocked at this confession. Albergio tells Dante that his sin was so terrible that the moment he committed it, he was taken out of his body and thrust here, and that a demon took the place of his soul in his worldly body. He names another person that Dante knows for certain is alive that this has also happened to, and Dante does not believe him, though the shade is convincing. Dante refuses to keep his promise to remove the frozen tears from the shade's eyes, saying that rudeness in Hell is a courtesy. Dante makes a plea to the city of Genoa about this sinner, telling them that they have a demon in their midst, and says that he wishes the whole lot of them driven from the Earth.

Commentary

Dante again invokes the Muses to help him write what he sees, just as he had done at the beginning of his journey. This time the invocation is longer and even more passionate. He knows that this portion of the journey is going to be harsh and horrible, and he hopes that he has the words for it.

Dante the Poet is fully aware that the noble art of poetry is not designed to describe the horrors of this dreadful abode. Poetry is not usually devoted to harsh and grating and vulgar sounds. Thus, he invokes the Muses of Poetry to help describe horrors in poetic terms.

The geography of the final pit of Hell is explained in these two cantos. There are four rounds in this circle of traitors. The first, Caina, reserved for those who were traitors to their kin, is named for the Biblical Cain who slew his brother, Abel. Remember also that Francesca (Canto V), in her story, says that Caina awaits hers and Paolo's murderer, Paolo's brother. The sinners that Dante finds there are two brothers who killed one another in a squabble over their inheritance, hence they must spend all of eternity locked together, bickering and butting heads.

Antenora is named for the Trojan Antenor who was believed to have betrayed Troy to the Greeks—this round is for those who were treacherous to their country. Here, Dante finds sinners deeper in the ice, unable to move their heads, and the sinner Bocca, a Florentine traitor, which reinforces Dante's political theme as well. Also residing here are Ugolino (a Guelph) and Ruggieri (a Ghibelline), both traitors to their country who conspired with each other to take over a certain faction of the Guelphs.

Ptolomea, named for those sinners treacherous to guests and hosts, is the third round. It is named after Ptolomey, a captain of Jericho and son-in-law of Simon the high priest. Ptolomey arranged a banquet honoring Simon and his two sons and then treacherously murdered them, while they were his guests. Here, the sinners lie supine with only their faces exposed, and here Dante discovers two sinners that were so treacherous to guests that they immediately were thrown out of their bodies and into Hell, and a demon was sent to inhabit their bodies on Earth. This action is contrary to Dante's idea of penitence to achieve Grace—these sinners did not have a chance to give penance, though it is apparent that Dante felt that this sin was bad enough to warrant immediate damnation.

The fourth and final round of the ninth circle, Judecca, is illustrated in the final canto. It is named after Judas Iscariot, who betrayed his lord and master, Jesus Christ.

Character Insight

Dante is indeed ready for the end of his journey. Twice in these cantos he shows no pity or sympathy for certain sinners; once, with a furious temper, he attacks one of the frozen spirits, simply for the satisfaction of knowing its name so he can tell his story on Earth. Unlike the spirits in the upper circles who ask to be remembered, the spirits in this part of Hell want to be forgotten because of their vicious crimes. If Dante treats theses spirits badly, he will show no compassion whatsoever because of the severity of their crimes on Earth.

The famous story of Count Ugolino gnawing on the head and brainpan of Archbishop Ruggieri is at the end of Canto XXXII. Historically, it was publicly known that Ugolino was captured and put to death by Ruggieri, but the manner of his death was so cruel that Dante thought the world should know the tragic story.

Dante, seeing the two bound together, wonders why Ugolino so beastly hungers after his neighbor.

Ugolino had been in prison for several months with his four young sons. One morning he awoke from a terrible dream and heard his children begging for food, and at the same time, he heard the doors of the tower being nailed shut. He knew this was the death knoll for him and his sons, and he had to watch them one by one cry out for food until they were all dead.

This eating and gnawing at flesh becomes central to "little Anselmo's" request to his father: "Thou didst clothe us with this wretched flesh, and it would be less painful if you eat of us." But of course Ugolino cannot eat of his own son's flesh. Then, as he sees each child die one by one, "starvation did what grieving could not do." Ugolino died and in Hell, is joined together with the enemy who starved his children and who now becomes the savage feast for him to munch on for eternity.

Dante cannot fathom what rage justifies such horrible and bestial actions, and he promises to reveal to the world the cause of Ugolino's savagery. Thus, he relates his story in Canto XXXIII from the viewpoint of the man who has been betrayed. By sympathizing with the victim, it is not apparent that Ugolino, himself, is a traitor who fully deserves his place in Hell. But, the four children are innocents and should not have become Ruggieri's victims. Furthermore, if Ugolino's hatred is so extreme, remember that no amount of punishment will satisfy his desire for revenge—it will never be satiated. He can never be revenged.

Ugolino's punishment is the concept of retaliation. This is a masterful stroke on Dante's part, for in the very depths of Hell, how else can Dante evoke pity for someone whose crime is as monstrous as was Ugolino's? Note, therefore, that Ugolino is here in Hell as a traitor because he betrayed his own party to Ruggieri, but also, that he is here in the poem as the betrayed. Ugolino may be said to be both the victim of divine justice and also the instrument of it, in that he also punishes his betrayer, Ruggieri.

It might be interesting to the historical-oriented mind that Ugolino was imprisoned with two middle-aged sons and two grandsons. But, this is history, and Dante changed the story to gain a more imaginative situation.

The law of retribution is the most powerful: In life Ruggieri starved Ugolino; in Hell, Ruggieri becomes food for his victim.

Glossary

Caina   the first round in Circle IX; named after Cain.

Foccaccia   murdered his cousin, causing a great feud between the Black and the White Guelphs.

Sassol Macheroni   appointed as guardian of his nephew and murdered him to get the inheritance.

Camicion de' Pazzi   murdered a kinsman.

Carlin   traitor to his country, will go to the next circle.

Antenora   second round of Circle IX.

Bocca   a Florentine traitor.

Buoso da Duera   accepted a political bribe.

Beccheria   abbot that plotted with the Ghibellines; the Guelphs cut off his head.

Gianni de' Soldanier   Ghibelline deserter.

Ganelon   infamous betrayer of his master Roland, Charlemagne's greatest warrior, in the French epic "Song of Roland."

Pisa   commune in Tuscany, Western Italy, on the Arno River.

Gualandi, Sismondi and Lanfranchi   Ghibelline nobles.

Friar Albergio   Jovial Friar; killed his brother at a banquet he hosted; the code was "bring in the fruit."

Atropos   *Greek and Roman Mythology.* the one of the three Fates who cuts the thread of life.

Branca D'Oria   Ghibelline who killed his father-in-law at a banquet he hosted.

Michael Zanche   father-in-law to Branca D'Oria; can be found in the sticky pitch of Canto XXII.

Canto XXXIV

Summary

The poets reach the final round of the last circle of Cocytus, the ninth and final circle of Hell called Judecca, and see the sinners there completely encased in the ice, in all sorts of strange and twisted positions. These are the sinners who were treacherous to their masters, and since they cannot speak, the poets move on to see Satan, the master of this place.

Dante uses Virgil as a windbreaker, because Satan's bat-like wings are flapping, creating a cold wind that freezes the ice firmer. Dante stands dazed and shaken in the presence of this hideous being and can only attempt to describe him.

Satan is bound in the ice to his mid-point and has three faces—a red one, a yellow one, and black one. In each of his three mouths he chews a sinner. Virgil explains that Judas Iscariot, who betrayed Christ, is the one in the middle and suffering most, and that the other two are Brutus and Cassius, who betrayed Caesar.

Virgil tells Dante to hold on to him as he climbs Satan's back, waiting for a moment when the wings are open so that they can have a safe passage down. Finally, Virgil climbs through a hole in the central rock, turning around—Dante is afraid that Virgil is going back through Hell, but both of the poets find themselves on their feet and standing on the other side of the world, having passed the mid-point of the Earth. They can see Satan's legs on this side, his body still frozen in the ice above.

Without pausing to rest, the poets make the long journey to the other side of the world where they are delivered though a round opening into the world under the stars.

Commentary

Theme

This final canto is the climax of the *Inferno*, the meeting with Satan. The sinners in this final round, Judecca (named after Judas Iscariot), keeping with the theme of retribution, are permanently frozen in the ice; they were treacherous to their masters, the ultimate sin of malice, and are forever encased in their sin of coldness.

Dante's two-fold theme of religion and politics is found in the very mouths of Satan. The ultimate sinners of this kind of malice spend eternity being chewed and flayed by Satan's teeth. The greatest sinner of the world is Judas Iscariot, the man who betrayed Jesus with a kiss. Both Brutus and Cassius betrayed Caesar, founder of Dante's beloved Roman Empire.

The image of Satan is a startling one, beginning with its three faces, which symbolize the perversion of the Holy Trinity. Dante says that Satan is as ugly as he was once beautiful, recalling his former incarnation as an angel. Satan, here, seems less powerful than traditionally depicted; he is dumb and roaring, trapped in the ice, punished as the rest of the sinners, perhaps worse.

Glossary

Beelzebub, Dis, Lucifer   Satan.

middle tierce   seven thirty.

CHARACTER ANALYSES

Dante

A Dante who has never sinned would have no need to make such a journey, because the object of the journey is, in part, to reveal to Dante the very nature of sin.

We never know what type of sin Dante has committed—this is not important—but, somewhere, he has simply strayed from the straight path. As he travels through this dreadful region, he retains those qualities that he has always possessed. And, he also displays a variety of emotions ranging from pleasure, to pity, to sympathy, to horror and revulsion.

For example, at the time of his journey, Dante was a rather well-known writer, and when he confronts the great classical writers whose greatness has survived the measure of time, he expresses awe merely to be in the presence of such greatness. Then, when the greatest poets of all time invite him to join them, this is a compliment of such high caliber that Dante's pride is heightened immeasurably.

In contrast, Dante soon meets a Glutton in Hell. Dante remembers him with pleasure. After all, Ciacco was a jovial and gracious host in life and was the typical "life of the party." Dante can only listen sympathetically to his condition. He feels so apologetic for not recognizing Ciacco that he fabricates an excuse so as not to hurt his feelings.

What endears Dante to the reader is his compassion for the sinners, even though he later comes to recognize that his pity is wasted upon them. Likewise, when he sees an enemy in Hell, such as Farinata, Dante is noble enough to recognize the power of the man, even while totally disagreeing with his political views. He sees Farinata as a strong majestic figure "towering" over Hell itself. He responds favorably to Farinata's love of Florence, especially when the sinner acknowledges that "maybe" he tested the city too much, but at least he was the one who kept his colleagues from razing the city to the ground. For this one act, Dante is proud to have met this powerful man and acknowledge his outstanding feats.

As he descends, he finds a beloved advisor, scholar, and fellow writer suffering, and his compassion is unsurpassed. He promises Brunetto Latini that his writings will be kept alive for all people to read and know. He departs from this wonderful teacher with tears in his eyes—it is one of the last times that Dante will weep for a sinner.

Dante, however, is not a one-sided person. He also has the power to respond to certain vicious sinners in a manner befitting their sins. When the wrathful person strikes out wildly, Dante has no pity and would possibly strike back. Then, in the ironic description of the sullen, Dante, for the first time, uses ridicule, and in the next circle he is seemingly pleased when the sufferings of Filippo Argenti are increased.

When a shade in the bottom of Hell refuses Dante's request for his name, Dante reaches out and uncharacteristically hurts the sinner by pulling out a tuft of his hair. Earlier, when he had inadvertently hurt the shade of a suicide, Pier delle Vigne, he feels deep remorse for injuring the sinner.

Virgil

Virgil displays all of the noble virtues attributed to the perfect Roman.

He represents reason and wisdom, making him the perfect guide. As the journey progresses, his treatment of Dante changes, depending on the situation. Often and most importantly, Virgil is very protective of Dante. At times, he reprimands Dante for his sympathy, reminding Dante that these dammed souls are here for punishment, and that their punishment is the design of a larger plan dictated by God.

Virgil is very careful to explain patiently all of the functions of Hell and its various structures. Virgil is constantly solicitous of Dante's welfare, and he knows that Dante is dependent on him. At times, when Virgil himself is having difficulty with some of the shades, he tells Dante to wait behind, because he does not want to frighten Dante, who is completely dependent upon him, as both a guide through the geography of Hell and as a spiritual guide.

Finally, even in the bottom parts of Hell, Virgil has to scold Dante for pitying those who deserve the punishment that they are receiving. Virgil's great task is to get Dante to harden his heart against the most horribly damned shades in Hell. He succeeds, and he shows Dante how to climb Lucifer's leg and then turn upright to see the stars of Purgatory ahead of him.

CRITICAL
ESSAYS

The Beginning and the Ending: Francesca and Ugolino

There are many discussions about the use of the number "three" and its various symbolic uses. But seldom is there any discussion of the number "two." However, looking at the beginning of Hell Proper and the ending of Hell Proper would demonstrate two contrasting pairs forever bound together.

Canto V, therefore, enters Hell Proper, which may be said to begin with the second circle, because here Minos is seated as the judge to determine where the sinners before him are sent for punishment. Thus, Hell Proper begins with Canto V and the punishment of Francesca and Paolo.

In contrast, Hell Proper closes with another pair—Count Ugolino and Ruggieri—locked in an embrace, with Ugolino gnawing on the brainpan of Ruggieri. Even though the final canto presents the horrors of being exposed to Satan itself, it is in the ending of Canto XXXII, where Dante first sees this gruesome pair, and in Canto XXXIII, where their story is told with such power and perfection, that Dante provides the thematic ending of Hell Proper.

Thus, Hell Proper begins with *love* joining two delicate souls together throughout eternity. In contrast, Hell Proper may be said to end with *hate* joining two violent, vicious men together throughout eternity.

Paolo and Francesca are bound together in a type of embrace and in a love that knows no bounds—a never-ending love that will continue throughout all eternity.

The other pair, Ugolino and Ruggieri, are at the bottom of Hell and are also bound together through a *hate* that can never be satiated—if anything, Ugolino's hatred will increase throughout all eternity.

It is also significant that their partners are not named and do not speak, but their presence is strongly felt during the narration. The partners do not speak because Paolo is enchanted with the manner in which Francesca defends their beautiful love. Ruggieri does not speak because the horror of his betrayal might cause even more torment. Furthermore, throughout this canto, it always seems that, at any moment, Ugolino will suddenly stop his narration and go back to his gnawing more fiercely than before.

Compare the introduction of both speakers: When Dante asks Francesca what brought her to this dreadful situation, she answers: "Thou shall see me speak and weep together" (V, line 26). And Ugolino says: "I will answer like one who weeps and tells" (XXXIII, line 26).

Francesca's answer includes her lover and the fact that as she speaks, they will both "weep together." Francesca and Paolo will weep together because of the difficulty it is, in such present misery, to recount such ultimate joy, as was their love for each other. Ugolino will weep, holding in his embrace the man whose evil caused him such ultimate pain and suffering.

Francesca is a fragile lady, guilty only of letting her overpowering love for Paolo become her sole desire. Love, love, love—so begins the three tercets describing her love for Paolo. Her speech has enormous, moving sincerity and beauty to it. "He loved me and I loved him!" And that is all. Never does she stoop to something so vulgar as to defend her love by saying something so mundane as: "Yes, but they tricked me, they betrayed me, I thought I was marrying the handsome Paolo with his beautiful body; instead, it was his ugly hunch-back vicious brother." This would not be her nature. She does not dwell on her betrayal because her essence is defined by her love and her essence is that of pure womanhood ("*l'essere gentile e puro*")—soft, pure, modest and tender— and in hell, she retains those qualities that inspired Paolo's love.

The mark of Hell is that the sinners retain those earthly qualities that condemned them. Francesca loved Paolo at first sight, loves him now, and will never cease to love him. Likewise, Ugolino hated Ruggieri in life, viciously hates him now, and no amount of hate and suffering will ever satisfy his desire for more and more hate.

Dante's genius is further seen in the fact that while Ugolino is in Hell for being a traitor, he is, instead, presented not as a traitor but as one who has been betrayed. The horror of his action is mitigated by the sufferings of a father. This is the law of retaliation: Ruggieri becomes the savage feast for the man who died of starvation along with his four sons. The horrifying image of Ugolino's savage repast is always before us—from the moment that Ugolino lifts his head from the "skull and other parts of the brain" and cleans his mouth by wiping off the "brain" matter, using his neighbor's hair as a napkin.

He, then, recites his tender narration of the horror of watching his four sons die one by one of starvation. Thus Ugolino hates violently because he loved his sons so intensely. His hatred is so great because his love was infinite, and his grief is so desperate because nothing can assuage him. As he finishes his story, he returns immediately to the gnawing of the brains and the crackling of the bones beneath him.

Both Francesca and Ugolino recollect the past with the same words, they both express their grief, and they both answer Dante's inquiries about their fate, but one emphasizes the controlling beauty of love, while the other dwells on the savage emotions of rage and hatred.

Dante the Poet and Dante the Pilgrim

Throughout the poem, there are two Dantes: Dante the Poet is a stern, moralistic individual who acts as the supreme judge and decides who belongs in Hell, and like Minos the monster judge, decides which circle of Hell each sinner belongs in. This Dante is unswerving in his judgment. He can find little extenuating circumstances, and the sinner is judged by the strictest and harshest standards.

For example, Dante the Poet lived in the household of the nephew of Francesca da Rimini, and he knew how she was betrayed in her marriage—how she was led to believe that her marriage was to be with the handsome and debonair young Paolo, but after her marriage, she discovered she was married to the deformed older brother. Her adultery was not a deliberate contrived matter; it was instead a gentle lapsing of the will; Yet, Dante the Poet places her in Hell. But Dante the Pilgrim swoons and faints when he hears her story in Hell.

Dante the Pilgrim is a man who has, himself, been lost in a dark wood, and he is sympathetic to others who have strayed from the right path. When he finds himself lost in the dark wood, he is terribly frightened, and when Virgil arrives, Dante the Pilgrim is at first apprehensive, cautious, and frightened until he is reassured of Virgil's noble intentions.

As they begin their journey, Dante shows all of the concern for the condemned that any humane, sympathetic person would show when confronted with the sufferings of the sinners. However, during his journey through Hell, Dante changes significantly as a pilgrim.

This change is first and most wonderfully exhibited when Dante and Virgil arrive in Limbo. When they approach the Circle of the Poets, Dante is invited to join them. Dante the Pilgrim is overwhelmed, as he should be, to be so honored and flattered by an invitation to join a group of the most outstanding and exalted poets of the world. Dante the Pilgrim feels unworthy to join this group, but, remember, it was Dante the Poet who issued the invitation. Thus, Dante the Poet, being invited to join these great classical poets, sees himself as one of their number. In reality, this could have been boastful on Dante's part or excessive pride, but fortunately, history has proved that he truly is one of the greatest of all poets.

And then as noted above, the reactions of both pilgrim and poet to the plight of Francesca present the same dichotomy of emotions—stern in judgment, but faint and swooning in emotional response.

The responses change only slightly when Dante confronts the Gluttons in the next circle. Ciacco, known as "the pig"—a common term in many languages for a Glutton—recognizes Dante the Pilgrim. Dante tries to recognize him, and failing that, he tries to assuage the feelings of this fellow Florentine by telling him that perhaps his "suffering" has changed his appearance. When Dante hears his name, he then remembers Ciacco as a "happy-go-lucky" fellow who was very pleasant and well liked. Dante treats him kindly and tells him, "Ciacco, your distress weighs upon me so that it moves me to tears." Again, remember it was Dante the Poet who chose him to represent the Gluttons. Thus, this far up in Hell, Dante is considerate for the feelings of the sinners and feels distress for the punishment they suffer.

However, Dante begins to lose some of his compassion beginning with Circle V. Here, the wrathful are striking at everyone, and Dante, as one strikes at him, defends himself. His behavior indicates that he is changing according to the nature of the sinners and their sins. How else could one respond to the wrathful and violent except in their own manner?

Through the lower parts of Hell, Dante is often fearful and constantly turns to Virgil for protection or for comfort. In addition to Dante's fear of the sinners in these lower circles, the Giants serve as another terror that Dante the Pilgrim must encounter and overcome. But he is reassured by Virgil. However, on some occasions, Dante becomes afraid when Virgil, himself, shows signs of confusion and weakness. Dante has to rely on Virgil, who symbolizes human reason and wisdom, to deliver him from Hell, and when his guide shows signs of failure or weakness, Dante the Pilgrim then becomes irritated and fearful. When Virgil is deceived by Malacoda, Dante the Pilgrim becomes confused about Virgil's qualities. But the reader should know that Dante the Poet causes this confusion, so as to illustrate the limitations and fallibility of pure reason.

Finally, when Dante reaches the ninth circle, Virgil upbraids Dante for pausing and weeping at these suffering shades. This is consistent with the hardening of Dante the Pilgrim's character in these later circles. There is no time for pure emotion at this point, the end of their journey is near; time is growing short, and Virgil must move Dante the Pilgrim along, even if this means that Virgil must take a harsher approach with Dante the Pilgrim. The reader must remember that Dante the Pilgrim is still utterly human and that his emotions change with each new encounter with a sinner, and Dante the Poet is forcing Dante the Pilgrim to realize that his pity does not change the fate of these sinners.

This change is complete when Dante the Pilgrim meets Bocca in the third round of Circle IX and accidentally kicks Bocca's head. He tries to get the shade to identify himself, but the shade refuses. Dante the Pilgrim then uncharacteristically pulls a tuft of hair out of Bocca's head, and his violence incurs no reproach because the ordinary forms of behavior are inapplicable here, among the completely depraved sinners where no punishment is enough for their horrible crimes.

But then, Dante comes to the final sinners, Ugolino and Ruggieri, deepest in the frozen lake of ice, with Ugolino gnawing on the head and brains of his companion. Here, however, Dante the Pilgrim only inquires, "Why do you show such a bestial appetite for your neighbor that you chew on him so ravenously?" Now, Dante the Poet steps in and lets it be known that whatever the causes for Ugolino gnawing so ravenously on "his neighbor," he will tell the story when he returns to the upper world.

Thus, one of the most horrible sinners in Hell gives a story that does not mention the reason for his punishment in Hell. Instead, it focuses on his betrayal and the punishment that he underwent at the hands of Ruggieri. With Dante the Poet telling this story, pity and fear and horror are all evoked. Thus, in the final part of Hell, the two Dantes are united. Note that the souls in upper Hell want to be remembered on Earth, while the souls in lower Hell are reluctant to even give Dante their names.

CliffsNotes Review

Use this CliffsNotes Review to test your understanding of the original text and reinforce what you've learned in this book. After you work through the review and essay questions, identify the quote section, and the fun and useful practice projects, you're well on your way to understanding a comprehensive and meaningful interpretation of the *Inferno*.

Q&A

1. How many circles does Dante's Hell have?

a. 7

b. 5

c. 11

d. 9

2. Why are many of the residents in Limbo there for eternity?

a. they were Gluttons

b. they were Treacherous to their Masters

c. they do not know the salvation of Christ

d. they sinned against Nature

3. Which of the following sinners is not in Satan's jaws?

a. Cassius

b. Brutus

c. Brunetto Latini

d. Judas

4. Dante's journey through Hell begins on Good Friday and ends on:

a. holy Saturday

b. Easter Sunday

c. Lent

d. The following Friday

5. At then end of the journey, when the poets reach the upper world, what do the poets see?

   a. a giant, shimmering mountain

   b. the stars

   c. another circle of Hell

   d. Beatrice

Answers: (1) d. (2) c. (3) c. (4) b. (5) b.

Identify the Quote

1. Midway in our life's journey, I went astray/from the straight road and woke to find myself/alone in a dark wood.

2. He will rise between Feltro and Feltro, and in him/shall be the resurrection and new day/of that sad Italy for which Nisus died . . .

3. "Are you there already, Boniface? Are you there/already?" he cried. "By several years the writ/has lied.

4. Joy to you, Florence, that your banners swell,/beating their proud wings over land and sea,/and that your name expands through all of Hell!

5. "Why do you kick me? If you were not sent/to wreak a further vengence for Montaperti,/why do you add this to my other torment?"

6. And I did not keep the promise that I had made,/for to be rude to him was a curtesy.

7. If he was once as beautiful as now/he is hideous, and still turned on his Maker,/well be he the source of every woe!

8. You are under the other hemisphere where you stand;/the sky above us is the half opposed/to that which canopies the great dry land.

Answers: (1) The opening of the *Inferno*, Canto I (2) Referencing Can Grande Della Scalla, Canto I (3) Said by Pope Nicholas III, mistaking Dante for Boniface, Canto XIX (4) Dante uttering scathing remarks about Florence, Canto XXVI (5) Said by Bocca, a traitor, after Dante accidentially kicks him in the head, Canto XXXII (6) After Dante promised to remove the ice from Friar Albergio's eyes but then refuses, Canto XXXIII (7) Describing Satan, Canto XXXIV (8) Virgil to Dante, explaining where they are after leaving the last circle of Hell, Canto XXXIV

Essay Questions

1. Describe Virgil's function in the *Inferno*. How does he differ from Dante? What does he represent? Is he an apt guide or could someone else have done better?

2. How does Dante grow as a character in the poem? How does his reaction toward sin change?

3. Dante wrote the *Inferno* partly as a warning to the people of Florence. Describe the political events of the time and how they affected this poem. What do some of the characters in the poem have to do with Dante's political views?

4. Descibe the nature of Divine Retribution and use examples from the text.

5. Why does Dante spend so much time on the eighth circle? What, in your opinion, were his motivations for spending thirteen cantos with those particular sinners?

Practice Projects

1. Some of the sins that Dante considered terrible, such as usury (banking), have become more accepted in modern culture. Draw a map of your own version of Hell, using "modern" sins. What do we consider "terrible" now that Dante may not have? What sins remain the same? Do some of the sins change circles? Next, place modern leaders, movie stars, and historical figures in your version of Hell and explain why you put them there.

2. Create a Web site that introduces readers to the *Inferno*. Focus, if you like, on one particular canto and explain, in detail, the significance included there.

3. Imagine that you are a traveler through Hell. In what circle, either Dante's or one you invent, would you be most inclined to spend eternity? Write a passage in *terza rima* describing the circle and your experience there. Do not forget to meet the souls that reside there.

4. In Canto IV, Dante meets and speaks with other great poets of antiquity and says that he "spoke of things as well omitted here/as it was sweet to touch on there." Write a passage of that imagined conversation. What would these poets say to one another? What do you think Dante asked them? What were their answers?

CliffsNotes Resource Center

The learning does not need to stop here. CliffsNotes Resource Center shows you the best of the best—links to the best information in print and online sources about the author and/or related works. Don't think that this is all we've prepared for you; we've put all kinds of pertinent information at www.cliffsnotes.com. Look for all the terrific resources at your favorite bookstore or local library and on the Internet. When you're online, make your first stop www.cliffsnotes.com where you'll find more incredibly useful information about Dante's *Divine Comedy: Inferno*.

Critical Works About Dante and the Poem

This CliffsNotes book, published by Hungry Minds, Inc., provides a meaningful interpretation of Dante's *Inferno*. If you are looking for information about the author and/or related works, check out these other publications:

Dante's The Divine Comedy: Modern Critical Interpretations, edited by Harold Bloom, offers current essays by some of the most well known names in modern criticism. Chelsea House Publishers: New York, Philadelphia. 1987.

Dante: Modern Critical Views, edited by Harold Bloom, offers thought-provoking contemporary criticism on Dante's work. Chelsea House Publishers: New York, Philadelphia. 1986.

Dante Alighieri: Twane's World Author Series, by Ricardo J. Quinones, offers an introduction to Dante's life and work, his influence and history, as well critical commentaries. Twane Publishers: Simon and Schuster/Macmillan, New York. 1998.

The Cambridge Companion to Dante, edited by Rachel Jacoff, provides an introduction to Dante that is accessible and challenging and includes fifteen essays by Dante scholars. Cambridge University Press: United Kingdom. 1993.

Dante Alighieri: Divine Comedy, Divine Spirituality, by Robert Royal, presents a reader friendly approach to the Divine Comedy as well as a biographical information. The Crossroad Publishing Company: New York. 1999.

Internet

Check out these Web resources for more information about Dante and *Inferno*:

The Dante Discussion Deck. `http://westerncanon.com/cgibin/lecture/Dantehall/mobydick.htm.`—A fun and informal site where you can post opinions, questions, even participate in live Dante chat.

Dante Divine Comedy Links and Dante Publications Online. `http://pages.ancientsites.com/~Torrey_Philemon/callipe/dante.html`—A variety of helpful links to essays, forums, chats, images, history, and texts. Also includes a fairly comprehensive list of links to Dante publications.

Dante on the Web. `http://www.geocities.com/1kurio/`—Great links, essays, text, images, current events, glossary, history, and more.

Digital Dante. `http://www.ilt.Columbia.edu/projects/dante/`—Hosted by Columbia University, this site is an academic research project that is reader friendly and comprehensive.

Electronic Bulletin of the Dante Society of America. `http://www.Princeton.edu/~dante/ebdsa.html`—Modern critical essays by contemporary Dante scholars and professors.

The World of Dante. `http://Jefferson.village.virginia.edu/dante`—Provides solid information and interesting pages, including one that allows you to search on words and characters occurring in the *Inferno* and one that allows you to generate a three-dimensional image of Hell.

Other Important Works By Dante

The dates of the writing of these books are approximate:

Vita nuova. 1292. This group of poems and commentary on them was written for Beatrice, Dante's true love.

De vulgari eloquentia. 1304-1307. A treatise on vernacular Italian, politics, religion, and poetry. Unfinished.

Convivio. 1304-1307. About the relationship between philosophy and political power. Unfinished.

De Monarchia. 1310. A book on Dante's political philosophies.

The Divine Comedy. 1306-1321. Epic poem that includes the *Inferno, Purgatorio*, and *Paradiso*. Dante's most famous work, completed just before his death.

Other Translations of Inferno

The *Inferno* is possibly one of the most widely translated poems ever written. This CliffsNote uses the popular John Ciardi Translation, though many other good translations are available, some can even be downloaded from the Internet. Here is a selection of modern translations:

Dante's Inferno: Translations by Twenty Contemporary Poets, edited by Daniel Halpern, offers the Inferno in a variety of modern poetic voices. Echo Press. 1999.

The Inferno of Dante: A New Verse Translation, by Robert Pinsky, gives a new and fresh voice to the Inferno, keeping the *terza rima* intact. Farrar, Strauss, and Giroux. 1995.

The Inferno, translated by Robert Hollander, a brand new translation. Doubleday. 2000.

The Divine Comedy, I. Inferno, Part I, translated by Charles Singleton, offers the poem in prose form. Princeton University Press. 1990.

Send Us Your Favorite Tips

In your quest for knowledge, have you ever experienced that sublime moment when you figure out a trick that saves time or trouble? If you've discovered a useful tip that helped you understand Dante's *Inferno* more effectively and you'd like to share it, the CliffsNotes staff would love to hear from you. Go to our Web site at www.cliffsnotes.com and click the Talk to Us button. If we select your tip, we may publish it as part of CliffsNotes Daily, our exciting, free e-mail newsletter. To find out more or to subscribe to a newsletter, go to www.cliffsnotes.com on the Web.

Index

NOTES

NOTES

NOTES